SATAN'S GIFT OF FEAR

SOME OF GOD'S PROMISES

John 10:29: *I will keep you safe because no one can snatch you out of my hand.*

Isaiah 40:11: *As a shepherd carries a lamb, I have carried you close to my heart.*

Psalm 91:7: *Thousands may fall around you, but you will not be harmed.*

Deuteronomy 1:30: *I will go before you and fight your battles.*

2 Timothy 2:13: *Even when weak in your faith, I will remain faithful to you.*

Psalm 23:3: *I will restore and refresh your weary soul.*

2 Corinthians 12:9: *My power will rest on you when you are weak.*

Psalm 40:5: *The good things that I have planned for you are too many to count.*

Exodus 14:14: *If you remain still, I will do your fighting for you.*

Psalm 37:4: *Delight in me and I will give you the longings of your heart.*

Hebrews 4:16: *Come boldly to my throne when you need to find mercy and grace.*

1 Corinthians 9:24: *An eternal crown awaits you at the finish line.*

1Kings 8:56: *Every word of every promise that I have made will come to pass.*

Romans 8:35-39: *Nothing in all creation will ever separate you from My love.*

Jeremiah 29:11: *My plan for your future is filled with hope.*

Psalm 119:105: *My word will brighten your steps and light your path.*

Isaiah 61:3: *I will give you beauty to replace your ashes.*

1 Corinthians 10:13: *I will not let you be tested beyond what you can endure.*

Revelation 3:21: *Those who overcome will sit with My Son on His throne.*

Joshua 1:9: Be *not dismayed: the Lord God is with thee withersoever thou goest.*

Proverbs 3:10: *So shall thy barns be filled with plenty; thy presses with new wine.*

Psalm 34:7: *The angel of the Lord encampeth round them and delivered them.*

Luke 22:33: *Heaven and earth shall pass away; but my words shall not pass away.*

The Why God Why Series

SATAN'S GIFT OF FEAR

Helen Glowacki

Cover photo by Nobby Natalie Clarke, Zwazulu-Natal, SA

Novels by Helen Glowacki
When God Broke Grandma's Heart
When God Took Grandma Home
When Grandma Chased the Spirits
The Granddaughter and the Monkey Swing
The Story of God's Plan of Salvation
God's Plan of Salvation: Tabletop Edition
Abiding Faith, Hidden Treasure
And Then They Asked God
Caleb's Testimony
As Evil Prevails (Coming soon)

Why God Why Series by Helen Glowacki
To What Purpose?
Why God Why?
Why Trust Scripture?
Life after Death And The Coming Tribulation
What Does God Want Me To Do RIGHT NOW?
Do Our Little Sins *Really* Count?
What Do Angels Do?
What is Faith?
Satan's Gift of Fear

Other non-fiction Books by Helen Glowacki
Politically Incorrect: When Enough is Enough
Overcoming Depression: How to be Happy
What No One Is Telling You about Addictions

****

Authors Website: www.helenglowacki.com

Face book: http://www.facebook.com/pages/The-Grandmother-Series/155300907853909?ref=ts and also http://www.facebook.com/pages/Helenglowacki/

The Why God Why Series

SATAN'S GIFT OF FEAR

Helen Glowacki

Cover photo by Nobby Natalie Clarke, Zwazulu-Natal, SA

HELEN GLOWACKI

Copyright © September 2013 by Helen Glowacki
Library of Congress Control Number:
ISBN   Hardcover
              Softcover: ISBN 978-0-9893-8078-2
              EBook ISBN

All rights reserved. No part of this book may be reproduced or transmitted in any form or by any means, electronic or mechanical, including photocopying, recording or by any information storage and retrieval system, without permission in writing from the copyright owner except in the case of brief quotations embodied in critical articles or reviews.

The novels by Helen Glowacki are works of fiction. References to real people, events, organizations, or locales are intended only to provide a sense of authenticity and are used fictionally. Characters, incidents and dialogue are drawn from the author's imagination and are not to be construed as real. Any resemblance to actual persons, living or dead is entirely coincidental.

The non-fiction books by Helen Glowacki represent the opinion, research, religious beliefs and scriptural interpretations of the author and not meant to be used in lieu of the advice of ministerial, theological, medical or psychological experts.

This book was printed in the United States of America. The King James Version (KJV) of the Bible, which is public domain in the United States of America, has been used for the scriptural references in this book.

The application of scripture is based on the opinion, the research and the religious beliefs of the author.

Cover assembly by Darren Robinson, dr Design & Associates, West Palm Beach, Florida, USA. Cover photo by Nobby Natalie Clarke, Zwazulu-Natal, South Africa.

For more information or to purchase this book, visit the authors website @ www.helenglowacki.com, visit the website of Amazon.com, or email the author at helen@helenglowacki.com

MISSION STATEMENT

To Serve

God

With All Our Strength

And

All Our Heart

Helen Glowacki

This book is dedicated to Wally

WHEN I MISS YOU THE MOST

When I miss you so much that my tears start to fall, I must trust even more that God oversees all.

His decisions are perfect even with heartbreak so deep, but when I forget this I can't my peace keep.

So I pray to my God asking help to withstand; I ask Him to cover me with His kind, loving hand.

And then though I miss you, the Lord eases my pain, and I see God's perfection so clearly again.

When I miss you I must remember God makes no mistakes; I must willingly walk the new path I'm to take.

For God took you before you suffered too much; He took you so gently with His loving touch.

You finished your journey and moved God's heart, and now you will rest for the short time we're apart.

Thus my task is to trust more, to grow and become the child that God seeks, because my work isn't done.

When I miss you I must remember God makes no mistake, and walk in thankfulness the new path I'm to take.

"Fear not for I am with you..."
Isaiah 41:10

ACKNOWLEDGEMENTS

Special thanks to my husband whose love and support has been the wind beneath my wings and a special gift from God. Thanks to my children and grandchildren for their sweet and gentle love and encouragement, and to Reverend Herold Ambroise for his many prayers on my behalf. Thanks to my dear friend Beth Jansen for her loving support and patient editing of this book.

My humble thanks to Ret. District Apostle Richard Freund (USA) for his encouragement and for the book reviews he has so graciously provided. Special thanks to the District Apostle Charles Ndandula (Zambia) for his many kindnesses and directives, and to the Henwood Foundation in Zambia for placing my books in their mission schools. Thanks to District Evangelist Ravishaq Bashir for distributing my books to the ministers, teachers and Sunday School children in the New Apostolic congregations he supports in Pakistan.

My thanks to Katharina Leipp of Muhlaker, Germany for the gift of her friendship and for translating my novel *Caleb's Testimony,* and the tabletop version of *The Story of God's Plan of Salvation,* and many of my articles into the German language. And thanks to Juan Cappurro for his generosity in translating *The Story of God's Plan of Salvation* into the Spanish language. These were a huge undertaking but allowed us to open our testimony to many other countries!

Thanks to Daniel Patrick Landolfi, Washington, DC for designing and maintaining my website. And thanks to Darren Robinson, West Palm Beach Florida for his meticulous assembly of the cover. Thanks to Nobby Natalie Clarke from

Enangeni, Kwazulu-Natal, South Africa for allowing me to use his beautiful photo for the cover of this book.

Thanks to Raphael Wyngaart for promoting my work and also for printing my articles in the Pretoria (South Africa) Newsletter, and thanks to Colette van Loggerenburg and others who have also supported and promoted my work throughout South Africa.

And special thanks to Richard Levinson for providing the first opportunity through which I could develop my writing skills; I will never forget that kindness and the many others you gave me.

Thanks to my brothers and sisters and ministers in faith who continuously shower me with their love and their prayers. And thanks to my Face book friends who support me every day in so many ways and pray for me so diligently. I am so grateful for your friendship, for encouraging me, and for sharing my work with others.

But most of all, my heartfelt, humble thanks to our Heavenly Father for His inspiration, guiding hand, protection, and never-ending love. May this work bring joy to His heart and may it touch a heart and help find that last soul!

NOTE TO THE READER

The King James Version (KJV) of the Bible, which is public domain in the United States, is used throughout all the books written by this author.

For further study, the author recommends the New King James Version (NKJV) of the Bible as easier reading and less usage of the old world language while remaining true to the original text.

The non-fiction books by Helen Glowacki represent the opinion, research, religious beliefs and scriptural interpretations of the author and are not meant to be used in lieu of the advice of ministerial, theological, medical or psychological experts.

The novels by Helen Glowacki are works of fiction. While some events in these novels reflect the expertise and support of those in particular vocations, references to real people, events, organizations, or locales are intended only to provide a sense of authenticity, and are used fictitiously.

Characters, incidents and dialogue are drawn from the author's imagination and are not to be construed as real.

Any resemblance to actual persons, living or dead is entirely coincidental.

No part of these books may be used or reproduced in any manner whatsoever without written permission except in the case of brief quotations embodied in critical articles and reviews.

MESSAGE FROM THE AUTHOR

As in many of our major life situations and important decisions, knowledge is power and ignorance is failure.... possibly even death. Spiritually it is the same. Spiritual knowledge requires work; it requires time and effort and practice to develop. Faith develops from the knowledge that God sees what we go through, hears our prayers and responds to us. It is *from this knowledge* that our faith can increase, our prayers can become more thankful, our fears and anxieties can dissolve, and a calm and patient expectation can be created in our heart. We learn to base our expectations not on an outcome *we* demand, but on the outcome God wants. Conversely, when we lack sufficient trust in God we continue to fall prey to fear and anxiety and become consumed by these emotions. Therefore, without learning why God has created a Plan of Salvation, why Satan tries to prevent us from learning God's words, why faith is so important, or why it will be tested, it is difficult to let go of our fears and to trust that **God is in control of *all* things, knows all things,** and has our best interest at heart.

A lack of spiritual knowledge prevents us from developing a close relationship with God and allows Satan to influence our lives. Without knowing God's Plan of Salvation and the part He asks us to play, we cannot prevent the ease with which Satan impacts the way we think and what we feel. Neither can we understand why he has the power and the desire to do so. Unless we know how and why he attacks in this manner, and why and where we may be vulnerable to such attacks, we cannot fight back. Without knowing God's plan, our quest for faith is a difficult challenge because our trust cannot increase, and our relationship with God does not grow into the intimate relationship we would like it to be. Further, **the peace we long for *cannot* withstand the**

onslaught it will receive under the satanic conditions we face. However, as we learn what God has provided for us we can begin to develop the wisdom to recognize and overcome these attacks. Therefore, God encourages us throughout all of scripture to *know* **Him**; to *learn* **of Him**; to *understand* **His goals** for us, and to *educate* **ourselves** as to why there are forces working against His Plan of Salvation. From books to bible study, from church services to television shows, from Christian magazines to friends, God provides numerous ways for us to learn.... even while running to and fro to satisfy our hectic schedules.

It is our human nature which allows fear and anxiety to overtake us when solutions to our difficulties are not immediately forthcoming. Yet, scripture tells us that faith can become so powerful that it can "move mountains". This tells us that sufficient faith can certainly remove fear and anxiety. Matthew 17:14-20 explains: "....... *If ye have faith as the grain of a mustard seed, ye shall say unto this mountain, Remove hence to yonder place; and it shall remove; and* ***nothing shall be impossible unto you****".* Scripture also tells us that we can ask for the peace which both our Heavenly Father and the Lord Jesus wish us to have. In fact, we can read throughout scripture the many ways in which God tells us **not** to be afraid. In Isaiah 41:10 we read: *"****Fear not****, for I am with you,* ***be not dismayed****, for I am your God. I will strengthen you,* ***I will help you****, I will uphold you with my righteous hand."* John 14:27 tells us: *"Peace **I leave** with you; my peace **I give** to you.....do not let your heart be troubled and* ***do not be afraid."*** Philippians 4:6 says: *"****Do not be anxious****, but in every situation, by prayer and supplication, with thanksgiving, present your petitions to God."* John 14:1 says: *"****Let not*** *your heart be troubled."* These are but a few of the hundreds of passages in the Holy Bible where God tells

His children that no matter what they go through, they need not be afraid. If we strive to remain faithful; learn His words; do our best to follow those words; and worthily participate in the sacraments God offers, He will never leave our side and will protect us despite what is occurring around us.

God wants to bless us and wants us to be joyful **even when we appear to be in jeopardy**, either emotionally or physically. He wants us to know and thereby trust that He is in control of everything. He understands that fear and anxiety can destroy us and can rob us of every joy and all hope. In fact, scripture tells us that faith also provides amazing health benefits. Proverbs 3:8 describes the effect of having faith in God's words by saying: *"It shall be **health** to the navel, and **marrow** to the bones."*

Sadly, long term anxiety can cause depression, lethargy and indecision. All of our reactions to fear can affect those around us because fear is contagious. While it isn't easy to fight the fear which Satan places in our hearts and minds, God does tell us how we can overcome it and rewards our effort to do so. In time, as we exercise our trust in God's help, that trust grows. God brings us through our difficulties and shows us over and over again that He can and will help us. God does not want us to carry the fear Satan brings us nor does he want it to be debilitating to us.

However, fear and anxiety have become one of the most prevalent problems in our society. According to the National Institute of Mental Health, in the United States alone, panic disorders affect over 6 million adults, Post Traumatic Stress Disorder affects over 7.7 million adults, and a generalized anxiety affects over 6.8 million adults. Statistics further indicate that anxiety causes a decline in one's daily performance and in one's health. Thus it is a problem well worth examining and well worth bringing under control, and fear is a problem which scripture clearly and often addresses.

When someone suffers greatly from anxiety and seeks the help of a physician many physicians will recommend prescription drugs to help allay their symptoms. Medication may be necessary when anxiety is caused by a chemical imbalance in the brain and/or long-term unending debilitating circumstances. But anxiety caused by a specific, short term and fixable problem may be better resolved with therapy. Medication is also considered a quick and easy fix for the discipline problems found in school children. Sadly, many school counselors place a mental health label on the children they counsel hoping that this will result in reducing their behavior problems. Labeling however often provides for both children and adults an **excuse** for certain behaviors by blaming them on uncontrollable anxiety or "deficits" which may or may not exist. In fact, it has been suggested that children placed on prescription drugs to temper behavior become adults who **rely** on medication to escape their problems and reduce the anxiety brought about by those problems. Labels and medications also become the basis for justifying the **dismissal** of a problem rather than encouraging one to face the hard work necessary to **remedy** it.

Interestingly, we can look to scripture to learn about fear and how to be free of the anxiety it produces. We also learn through scripture that the Adam-like nature must be subdued in order for us to succeed spiritually. This requires change and takes time, effort and self discipline. Adding to this dilemma are the demands which today's society makes on all of us which exhaust the time required to learn scripture. Busy schedules pull us away from God's word and *encourage* us to look instead for an easy, and **immediate** solution. Our impatient Adam-like nature, seeking immediate gratification, makes it difficult to properly research and apply what scripture recommends. This compounds our anxiety and creates an overwhelming fear which works to weaken us and make us lethargic and complacent. Scripture tells us that faith is the substance of things hoped for, the evidence of things not seen. For many, without the substantive and **immediate** evidence we desire, we don't look ahead. We don't realize that God has the answer for all our concerns. We do not recognize that long term dependency on many of the drugs used for anxiety can cause us to lose focus on God's instruction...which is exactly what Satan wants. Satan's goal is to plant doubt and confusion into the minds of the children of God in order to separate them from God's instruction. **Anxiety and drug dependency are a perfect platform through which Satan can accomplish this goal.**

Despite the work that Satan does in our lives, we have an omnipotent, caring Heavenly Father who loves and protects us. The greater our understanding of God's help and power, the more we trust His ways and His help, and the less we fall captive to the fear, anxiety and hopelessness Satan brings. Sadly, the main obstacle to tapping in to what God provides for us is the exhaustion caused by our busy schedules and the added anxiety those schedules bring. This is compounded by the medications prescribed to help reduce our anxiety. **These work together to inhibit our desire and ability to study God's words.** Scripture warns that lacking sufficient knowledge of God's plan can be detrimental to our soul salvation. In fact, Hosea 4:6 tells us: *"My people are destroyed for lack of knowledge.....".* This teaches us that God foresees that we will no longer learn what He offers, how He helps, and why the Plan of Salvation was instituted for our benefit. Nor will we learn that Satan works against God and against God's children to prevent us from learning what God wants to tell us. Yet scripture teaches us that our Heavenly Father **does** help and **can heal all things** and teaches us **how** we can fight back to overcome the traps which Satan lays for us.

Trusting God provides an incredible soothing effect on every part of our being. It is through learning God's words and learning of His Plan of Salvation that we can develop trust. It is comforting to know that God wants us to have peace in our hearts and will always protect us. Therefore this book seeks to provide that information by offering short, concise explanations of the many and various parts of God's Plan for us, of the help God offers, and why we must be aware of what Satan does. Gathering God's words on this subject has reinforced my own beliefs and taught me what to do when troubling times bring the instant reaction of fear and anxiety. Thus writing this book has been cathartic for me and has helped me on the road to overcoming my own fears. I hope that this book will assist many who suffer from fear and anxiety at least as much as it has helped me.

If you enjoy this book, please look for the other titles in my *"Why God Why"* series which address the many and varied concerns we face in life. And, if you feel that these words have given you hope and direction, please share what you learn with others for there are many who suffer needlessly *"for lack of knowledge"!* May God open your understanding of His words and may He bless you and keep you always.

Helen Glowacki

TABLE OF CONTENTS

Dedication	Page	08
Acknowledgements	Page	09
Message from the Author	Page	11
Table of Contents	Page	19
Chapter 1: The Adam-Like Nature	Page	21
Chapter 2: Why We're Fearful	Page	29
Chapter 3: Satan's Goal	Page	37
Chapter 4: Climbing The Mountain	Page	43
Chapter 5: Losing What We Love	Page	49
Chapter 6: How Do I Learn to Trust God?	Page	57
Chapter 7: Just Say "No"	Page	65
Chapter 8: Patience	Page	71
Chapter 9: Getting Right With God	Page	79
Chapter 10: The Overcomer	Page	91
Bibliography	Page	99
About the Author	Page	101
Excerpt from *What Do Angels Do?*	Page	103
Synopsis of this Authors Books	Page	109
Book Reviews	Page	115

"…..do not be anxious…. but….. by prayer and supplication….. present your petitions to God."

Philippians 4:6

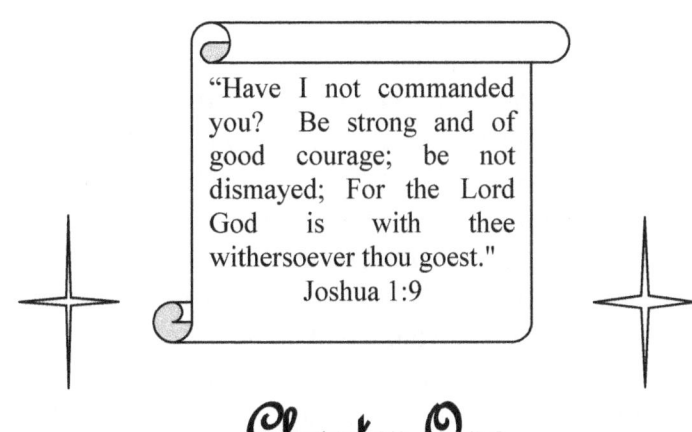

"Have I not commanded you? Be strong and of good courage; be not dismayed; For the Lord God is with thee withersoever thou goest."
Joshua 1:9

Chapter One

THE ADAM-LIKE NATURE

It can be humbling to admit that we allow our fears to overtake us especially when we understand that if we *truly trusted* God we would not be fearful. It is embarrassing to admit that while we may know what scripture tells us to do, think, or feel about our concerns, we don't follow the advice we have been given. It hurts our pride to acknowledge our failure because it is an admission that we have not developed the self-control and determination to become the person God wants us to be. Even when we admit that it is through grace that we find the strength to change our Adam-like nature and become more like Christ in our trust and obedience to God, we find it difficult to face the fact that we do not have **enough** knowledge about, nor **enough** trust in God to help us make these changes. Added to this dilemma is our lack of patience. Yet a change in behavior **requires** patience if we expect our efforts toward change to bear fruit. We cannot fight fear and obtain peace without an understanding of what scripture tells us, and without an understanding of Satan's goals. Luke 6:44 tells us: *"Each tree is recognized by its own fruit."* Therefore, we **know** that we are not trusting God by the simple fact that **we allow our fears to overshadow our lives.** When fear reigns in our bodies **for any length of time** we must acknowledge that **we have failed** the test of faith. When fear overtakes us we are **not** producing the proper "fruits" from God's words but falling back on our **own** resources. This allows Satan to have the upper hand. This in itself can be daunting and prevent us from moving forward and being the "overcomer" God encourages us to become. We allow ourselves to be so overwhelmed by our fears that at times it seems easier to curl into the fetal position hoping that our cross will fade away on its own. Thus **we sabotage our own happiness.** But this isn't what God asks of us or wants for us. He wants us to be fearless; to be warriors; to fight what Satan tries to do.... and He promises to help us in the process. When we **do** finally learn how to engage in fighting back....the reward can be...in time.... complete freedom from fear. **But, how can we accomplish this? How do we get past the lethargy, the pain, the anxiety, the repeat patterns, our lack of knowledge, and our defeatist attitude?** How can we examine the situations which impact our here and now **and** our eternal future and come up with a solution? Where can we obtain the strength and the wisdom to accomplish this?

God promises to lift the veil from our eyes and open our understanding to His truths if we ask Him to help us and are willing to work toward that goal. He promises to help us mentally, physically, emotionally and spiritually. He promises us throughout scripture that **we do not have to be afraid**; that **we can trust Him**, and even test Him. So, a good place to start our journey of overcoming our fear would be to explain our situation to our Heavenly Father through prayer and ask Him to help us learn **what** He asks of us and **why,** and to help us recognize and avoid the subtle traps which Satan lays for us. We must tell Him that **we truly *desire* to trust Him** and are willing to read and believe His words and promises. We must tell Him that **we *desire* to believe** and thus overcome our fear but that **we need help** to discern those spirits of fear, learn what God wants us to do, and take the action He suggests. Sadly however, we don't pray in this fashion; **we don't have *"enough"* faith** to believe that we **can** be helped; we succumb to our fears; and we are too lethargic to put in the effort it takes to be helped. Therefore, we fall prey to the false input Satan places in our hearts and minds which whispers that since God hasn't *already* helped us, He probably won't.... and we are overwhelmed. Satan also "reminds" us that our fears and anxieties exist because we deserve punishment for our daily faults and failings...and those of the past. He also causes us to believe that we do not need to heed the advice of scripture. Instead Satan tells us that we must implement **our own** source of relief, even though this has never in the past brought the relief or change we desire. Satan causes these misconceptions to enter our heart and soul because we make judgments about our situation with only a **small amount of information and absolutely no patience, perseverance or trust, and very little knowledge about God.** We fall into Satan's hands because **the emotions we are experiencing *and allowing* are painful. We want them to end NOW, and when they don't, we give up and we suffer. We may turn to medication or whatever other course of action might promise immediate relief!** God has given us the scriptures so we can learn; so we can recognize the ploys Satan uses to trap us. God wants us to compare satanic rhetoric to what God tells us through scripture. But this can't be done overnight.

Scripture teaches us that **the end times, the times in which we now live, will bring great tribulation to the**

children of God and shake their faith. Scripture teaches that its **words are God's words and therefore *truth* and that they can be used to fight the work of Satan!** Scripture teaches us not to allow the pain of fear and anxiety to make us stop trusting God. It tells us that ***everything*** which occurs, God sees and that He can bring a blessing from it. It explains that we must ask ourselves if what **we endorse** is godly; if what **we support** is pleasing to God and if what **we do** is beneficial to our soul salvation. We must also ask whether or not **we are *willing*** to **fight against what does not fit that criteria.** Satan is never blatant. He is subtle and clever, and usually unobtrusive...**Satan *does not want to be discovered*...**and, he is delighted when we fall prey to the fear he places in our hearts. He knows that **when we believe his lies, and lose our faith in God's help, he will gain time** to wreak more havoc on the children of God. He knows too that this will help him remain free from the Lake of Fire where he will be bound once God's Plan of Salvation is complete and the last soul God longs for has been made ready. God's Plan of Salvation **will** move forward and **will not** be hampered by what Satan does, ***but we can be affected by the work of Satan as our faith is tested.*** Therefore we must watch, and must **seek the knowledge** we need to ***recognize how Satan works,*** and where and through whom he works, and...... what actions **we must take** to become and remain a faithful child of God. We must **use** the tools God offers and must view our Adam-like nature the way we view the training of a very young child. To control the impulses of our Adam-like nature, we must **learn** what God says, and then we must **work** to deny the impulses of that nature and **direct** our thoughts toward godly reactions and behaviors. This takes time. **One** rebuke, **one** instruction is not enough. To overcome this nature, one lesson is not enough; many lessons... much patience.... and perseverance is needed to succeed....thus it is similar to teaching a small child. This process may require five lessons, or ten or twenty depending upon our willingness to learn and depending upon where we are in our spiritual development... **and it will also depend upon how much we <u>want</u> to change.** Sadly, we don't know when our lessons will end or when we will have **internalized** what God wants of us and the instruction He gives to help us. God, in His loving kindness does not test our faith without first giving us the opportunity to learn what will help us pass this test. Satan works to blind us to the truth and hamper us from understanding and implementing what will help us. Our experience and subsequent reaction will not only be a test of faith, but will measure the development of our Christ-like nature. Passing this test means that we can go on with our life **free of fear** and **filled with trust** in God!

God tells us that there is an incredible reward when we come to Him, listen, learn, and **decide with our own free will** to initiate and accept His direction for our lives. To the faithful, to ignore God's incredible offer is beyond comprehension when so much is at stake, especially when one learns what will happen to those who will be, in the end, rejected by God because of their rejection of Him. Yet we cling stubbornly to the Adam-like nature rather than risk the work of leaving it behind for the Christ-like nature. Sadly, what is most familiar to us feels, **temporarily**...better. Therefore, as we begin the effort to make a change, it is often very uncomfortable. But the bottom line is that those who love God are those who are willing to work to **discard the Adam-like nature** which wants its own way, is easily swayed by Satan, is impatient, and repeats the same debilitating patterns over and over again. God makes an incredibly beautiful promise to us in 1 John 3:9-14: *"The Lord is not slack concerning his promise, as some men count slackness; but is longsuffering to us-ward, not willing that any should* *perish, but that all should come to repentance.* But **the day of the Lord will come as a thief in the night;** *in which the heavens shall pass away with a great noise, and the elements shall melt with fervent heat, the earth also and the works that are therein shall be burned up. Seeing then that all these things shall be dissolved,* **what manner of persons ought ye to be** *in all holy conversation and godliness. Looking for and hasting unto the coming of the day of God, wherein the heavens being on fire shall be dissolved, and the elements shall melt with fervent heat? Nevertheless we, according to his promise,* **look for new heavens and a new earth, wherein dwelleth righteousness.** *Wherefore, beloved,* **seeing that ye look for such things, be diligent that ye may be found of him in peace, without spot, blameless.** " What we learn from this is to think of change the same way that we think of going to school. We may have to work very hard for a few semesters, but the end result is the degree we receive which allows us to pursue our dream! We alone decide whether or not we are willing to do the work which acquiring such a degree demands. Sadly, no one can do it for us. But by surrounding ourselves with those who will teach us, encourage us, lift us up and re-direct us when we begin to fail, strengthen us as we try to get back on track, and set an example to pray, offer, love, trust and be patient.... we will emerge a winner! It is an added bonus when those who once suffered from fear and anxiety themselves **help us change** *our* **fear response**. Therefore when a child of God has overcome the debilitating ploy of fear which Satan loves to use, God asks that they help others in the process of overcoming that fear. It is comforting to receive help from those who have experienced what we have, and have overcome it. They "understand" how difficult it is! But with our human nature embroiled in the Adam-like nature, it is often easier to let things slide, or to try to hide our weakness or simply deny it. And sadly, the Adam-like nature has the ability to *justify* our complacency, our "do it tomorrow" attitude, and justify the pride which won't let us admit our failings to others.

It is also through the Adam-like nature that we find an excuse to turn back from the process of change when we see that our **first attempts to do so are difficult** and painful. Making the necessary changes in our life does not occur overnight. Those who have gone through this process understand that to help us, they need to continue to push us, they need to admonish us, and thereby risk our anger. God wants us to stand up for what He teaches us in scripture and to admonish against every nuance of sin so that we help others learn what is displeasing to God and **what brings us harm.** Our task as children of God is to rebuke and admonish those we love, and to explain the process of freeing ourselves from the fallen spirits which bring us into sin...and fear. Even the early Apostles were taught to teach, to rebuke, to admonish and to unequivocally state what God wanted them to tell the people. With our desire for instant gratification and our need to be liked by everyone, it is difficult to admonish. We sometimes give in to "flattering" words so that we do not sound "burdensome" by harping on Satan's work, or when we face "contention" as we try to share God's words. It is difficult to speak the absolute truth when rebuking sin while also trying to be gentle, and to "cherish" the children of God during this effort. The Apostles too had to learn to open their souls to whomever they brought the word of God and face the anger of those they wanted to help. Scripture describes how painful it was for them as they were buffeted by those who did not like their message and tells us that **they were "shamefully entreated"** when they were bold in bringing God's words and statutes to the people. These Apostles knew that it was their duty to teach God's truth to help one another be worthy when Christ returns. We can read in 1 Thessalonians 2:1-13 how the early apostles fulfilled their duty to God and to His children and addresses some of the difficulties in doing so. *"For yourselves, brethren, know our entrance in unto you, that it was not in vain: But even after that we had **suffered** before, and **were shamefully entreated,** as ye know, at Philippi, we were bold in our God to speak unto you the gospel of God with **much contention.** For our exhortation was not of deceit, nor of uncleanness, nor in guile; But as we were allowed of God to be put in trust with the gospel, even so we speak; **not as pleasing men,** but God, which trieth our hearts. For **neither at any time used we flattering words,** as ye know, nor a cloak of covetousness; God is witness; **Nor of men sought we glory, neither of you, nor yet of others, when we might have been burdensome,** as the apostles of Christ. But **we were gentle** among you, even as a nurse cherisheth her children; So being affectionately desirous of you, we were willing to have imparted unto you, not the gospel of God only, but also our own souls, **because ye were dear unto us**. For ye remember brethren, our labor **and travail**: for laboring night and day, because we would not be chargeable unto any of you, we preached unto to you the gospel of God. Ye are witnesses, and God also, how holily and justly and unblameably we behaved ourselves among you that believe; As ye know how **we exhorted** and comforted **and charged** every one of you, as a father doth his children. That ye would walk worthy of God, who hath called you unto his kingdom and his glory. For this cause also thank God without ceasing, because when ye received the word of God which ye heard **of us**, ye received it not as the word of men, but as it is in truth, the word of God, which effectually worketh also in you that believe."* But, ultimately it is up to us to ask for, to seek, and to accept the help which is offered.

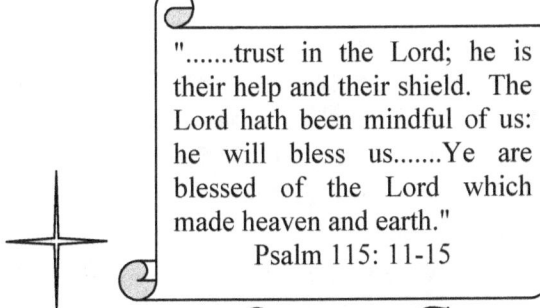

"……trust in the Lord; he is their help and their shield. The Lord hath been mindful of us: he will bless us……Ye are blessed of the Lord which made heaven and earth."
Psalm 115: 11-15

Chapter Two

WHY WE ARE FEARFUL

When Adam and Eve sinned they lost the relationship they had with God. But God, knowing that this would occur, had prepared a way for mankind to return to Him. Because man fell to the wiles of Satan through their sin, God placed into the natural protective instincts of mankind, a nervous system response which would sense danger, and prepare the body to either flee a situation or stand and fight. This instinct is called the "fight or flight syndrome". It is activated by a sense of danger which causes the release of adrenalin. Adrenalin alerts the body to a potential threat and provides the strength to take immediate action. Incredible feats of heroism, often requiring an inordinate amount of physical strength, have been recorded to occur during the release of this hormone. This accounts for those times when a single person can do more than is possible under ordinary circumstances. For example, when one can singlehandedly lift a burning car to allow the car's occupant to escape, it is adrenaline which provides the strength required to do so. The flight or fight mechanism, which God placed into our bodies, helps us survive as a species by warning us of danger and by giving us the instinct and the strength to take action to deal with that danger. When adrenalin is released, another hormone called nor-epinephrine is also released which augments our preparation for fight or flight by shifting blood from the central part of the body to the extremities. This creates a readiness to fight or flee. The body then goes through a series of events after which Cortisol is finally released. This steroid hormone maintains fluid balance and blood pressure. However, while these hormones are effective in an emergency, *they **can be detrimental to our health if they remain present in the body for too long a period of time.*** Cortisol, which is better known as Hydrocortisone, can cause inflammation in various parts of the body and has been found to be one of the underlying causes of heart disease, arthritis, cancer and other serious health problems. Cortisol can also suppress the immune system, increase sugar, decrease libido and contribute to obesity. Thus, **when God tells us not to fear** and reminds us to trust Him and seek His peace, He is not only teaching us how to live a contented life, but also ***helping us avoid the debilitating effects which carrying our fear may have on our bodies. This shows us what measures God has taken to protect us! It also shows us the importance of trusting Him!***

Medical research into the "Flight or Fight Syndrome", and illnesses such as Post Traumatic Stress Syndrome and other anxieties resulting from fear, have given us great insight into the physiological responses which occur when fear is present. Scripture tells us that **fear robs us of our ability to trust that God will see us through all circumstances and that without that trust a life of havoc will instead direct our responses to our concerns.** But, scripture also teaches us about another very dangerous influence which can cause us to fear and use our fear to direct our every day decisions. Scripture explains that Satan and his helpers work day and night to instill fear in the children of God because **when we are afraid, we become susceptible to Satan's guidance.**

SATAN'S GIFT OF FEAR

Amazingly, scripture warns that fear itself brings a snare to men. Proverbs 29:25 tells us: *"The fear of man bringeth a snare, but whoso putteth his trust in the Lord shall be safe."* A snare is a trap, and a trap is a mechanism which holds us prisoner. This tells us that **we are held against our will by the reaction which occurs in our bodies from the fear that Satan instills in us.** We react and over-react, and we take action that is not well thought out. It is through our lack of faith that **Satan** exercises his power and **"conditions" us to react to our circumstances with fear and anxiety.**

There are three major parts to the brain. The lower part of the brain or **Brain Stem** acts without requiring any thought from us. It causes our heart to beat and our lungs to breathe without a conscious order from us to do so. The **Mid Brain**, which is our fear center, is both instinctive and reactive. It contains the **amygdala** which responds on an "all or nothing" principle which it bases on a *perceived* threat. The amygdala can be conditioned. Therefore it's response often over-rides common sense. Finally, the **Neo-Cortex** is where reason and logic take precedence to solve problems. This area of the brain will often try to send the amygdala the message to stop its fear response.

God teaches us through scripture how we can stop fear. But when we are caught in the trap of our fear, it is in this final connection in the Neo-Cortex where something has gone wrong; thus this is where Satan has penetrated our defenses. If we study this phenomenon from a Biblical point of view we discover that this may be one of the reasons why our Heavenly Father asks that we overcome our Adam-like nature and become more Christ-like in nature. The "Adam" brain constantly searches for information from which it can *instinctively* obtain safety or pleasure. Therefore the "Adam" brain is extremely susceptible to outside influences. When the amygdala perceives a threat it sends a message to the hypothalamus that there is danger. The hypothalamus then releases CRH which is the messenger it sends to the pituitary gland. When the pituitary gland is alerted to danger it will release ACTH which acts as its messenger and sent to the adrenal glands. The adrenal glands response is to produce Cortisol which will maintain the fluid balance and blood pressure in the body. However, Cortisol is very harmful when constantly released into our tissues and often shows up in lab tests as an inflammation marker. Those who suffer from panic attacks should have the inflammation markers of the body checked on a regular basis.

In most cases we learn to avoid what causes us anxiety. But when we face our fears **rather than avoid them**, and we confront them instead of denying them, a process which is called "exposure" takes place. Exposure often works...in time.... to quell fear because the amygdala *can be taught* to either panic or not. For instance, the smell of chocolate chip cookies emerging from the oven will not cause panic because **we have learned** how pleasant these can be by being exposed to its benefits. But if we have been bitten by an angry dog in the past, suddenly hearing and seeing a dog running toward us will cause the amygdala to panic. This is because **we have been "conditioned"** to *believe* that a snarling dog can bring us harm. Thus this situation triggers an immediate "panic" type reaction. Because what we see, feel, hear or smell is sometimes pleasant (eating the chocolate chip cookie), and at other times is unpleasant (the possible assault of an angry dog), our brain will categorize what we face and react in a similar manner **with each encounter**. This reaction is **based upon our perception** of whether or not our experience was pleasant or unpleasant. Based on this information we can see how **easily we become susceptible to fear**. When we again encounter a situation which might bring us a similar unpleasant or painful circumstance, we feel anxiety and the desire to avoid that situation. Therefore, because we rely on a **negative past experience** in every similar situation, we have a very difficult time in "reconditioning" the amygdala to the point where it will allow the Neo-Cortex to shut down the fear response. Therefore **we continue to suffer** and experience an increased heart rate, sweating, dry mouth and oxygen deprivation to the digestive system. The Cortisol release which occurs continues now on a **regular basis** and becomes harmful to us.

Satan, fully understands our natural (Adam-like) inclinations and makes use of this information. He gleefully looks for our weakest points through which he can wreak his havoc on our lives. His greatest joy is to make us fearful. He knows that **fear can immobilize us, make us lose hope, make us blame God for our circumstances, make us sick, and can take away the energy we need to learn God's words. Fear is a *driving* force; a force which *impels* us to seek a way out of the circumstance we fear.** Satan knows that **fear can lead us into sin and prevent us from trusting God.** Fear also makes us so tired that we find no time or energy to learn God's words or seek His offer of comfort and direction. Fear can cause us to retreat from making decisions and seeking help. Fear therefore contributes to us **becoming isolated and devoid of the resources we need** to be helped. So **how can we reduce our fear? The answer is to trust God. But, how do we trust *enough* to banish this terrible influence in our lives?** Many try and most fail, but why? When we read the parable of the five wise and the five foolish virgins in Matthew 25:1-13, it tells us that all ten virgins were faithful, believed that Christ would come for them, were dutifully waiting for Him, and expected to go with Him. When we ask ourselves *why* the five foolish were left behind and what made them different than the five wise virgins, we learn that the five foolish virgins had not filled their lamps with oil and at the last minute ran to obtain what they needed. Though they obtained the oil, it was too late; the Lord had left without them. When scripture refers to the oil required to keep a lamp lit it is reminding us of our need for the "light" of understanding which comes God's words. Without filling our hearts and minds with the word of God, and our soul with the forgiveness Christ offers, we may not find our way through the darkness of evil which works day and night to prevent us from becoming those who God will bring into His new kingdom. But what this also means is that **without this understanding, Satan can wreak havoc on our minds and our bodies.** Christ's sacrifice allows the forgiveness of our sins but it is God's words which teach us how to protect ourselves from the power which Satan wields. Sadly, few of us ask if we truly "know" God; if we know **what** He plans, **what** He offers, and **what** we need to do to be a part of His new kingdom. Without this knowledge we cannot learn what will help us fight against Satan and his fallen angels. While God will bring to all who were ever conceived, born or died the same opportunity to learn of Him and become a part of His new kingdom....not everyone will accept. While this may deny them a future with God, it also condemns them to a life of fear if they become one of Satan's targets. Fear is not only that which we recognize as a danger, but fear is also why we feel "outside" social gatherings, or feel "not ready" to enter into a close relationship with anyone, or cannot make decisions. Fear can be that which we recognize and cower from, but **it can also be what we never see yet we react to very strongly** on an internal level both mentally and emotionally. Some of the words used by Webster's Dictionary to define the word "fear" are: *afraid, apprehensive, aware of danger, anxious, alarmed, agitated, panic, terror, dread, and trepidation.* None of these words represent something we would invite into our lives. So, how do we avoid them? Hosea 4:6, tells us that we may be barred from God's new kingdom because we do not know what is required of us. This verse states: *"My people are destroyed for lack of knowledge, because **thou has rejected knowledge**, I will also reject thee that thou shalt be no priest to me, seeing that thou hast forgotten the law of thy God, I will also forget my children."* This tells us that God realizes that many are not aware of His Plan of Salvation and therefore not applying His admonitions to every decision and every choice they make as they move through their daily lives. Therefore **they cannot believe** the promise God makes to care for them, nor Christ's sacrifice to free them of sin. This tells us that we cannot be a part of the work of God if we do not have an understanding of how we are to discern the spirits, how we are to accept or reject what we see and hear, how we should decide what actions to take, and what to accept as truth. Our natural lives bring us the difficulties of time constraints, stress, exhaustion, and challenges which distract us from the more important issue of our soul salvation. These provide us with an excuse (justification) **not** to study what scripture tells us...or to study just a little and take it out of context so we can negate the need to learn more. Sadly, this takes away our ability to live a life filled with joy and hope, and one which **does not allow fear to dictate** what we do and say and think. We, in essence do the very same thing which Adam and Eve did when they believed what Satan told them. When Satan came to them in the Garden of Eden they had no idea that he was evil incarnate; they were influenced by his beauty and his softly spoken words. They were amazed by how **he made them think differently** than they had before he spoke to them. He planted an arrogance of thought into their minds which made them wonder whether or not God's warning was really paramount. Satan **beguiled** them into doing what God had clearly said they should not do. Yet despite our understanding of what happened to Adam and Eve and what scripture teaches, few of us desire to learn more about Satan or about why and how he works against us and against God's plan for our future. Yet it is **because of Satan's influence on us** that few of us compare what we hear in this world to what God tells us. Few of us watch for beguiling words which subtly negate the principles upon which God wants His children to build their future. Therefore we succumb to fear. We do not understand that **Satan is a powerful entity who works in our lives every day,** or that scripture tells us that Satan is a liar, beguiles us, uses men to harm us, tempts us, rewards evil, and works day and night to prevent God's Plan of Salvation from coming to fruition. **When we ignore the power and consequences of these facts we are gambling with our eternal life.** What does it cost us to investigate God's plan and open ourselves to godly wisdom? When we ignore or negate what God wants us to learn we are gambling with the loss of a *good* life here on earth and **dooming ourselves to the fears which Satan so subtly instills in our heart.** Trusting God brings peace and comfort, but few of us can attain that without immersing ourselves, *our brain*, in what God tells us and.... following His advice.

Reading the story about Daniel being forced to spend the night in a lion's den where everyone thought he would be devoured by the lions, or the story of Shadrach, Meshach, and Abednego who were forced to enter a blazing furnace which burned everything inside it within minutes, or the story of what Job had to endure when Satan took everything he loved away from him in the hope of making him blame God, helps us see what knowing God's words and having faith in them can do. But, because **this is so much harder to do than to know,** the question remains: How can we accomplish this in our lives?

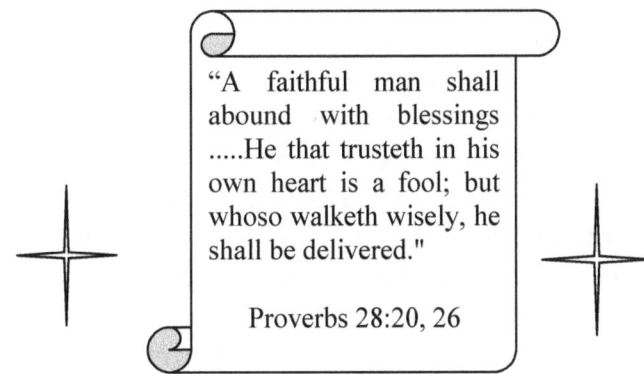

"A faithful man shall abound with blessings .....He that trusteth in his own heart is a fool; but whoso walketh wisely, he shall be delivered."

Proverbs 28:20, 26

Chapter Three

CLIMBING THE MOUNTAIN

Because we live in a time where political correctness often inhibits discussions of religion and politics, we seldom hear about spiritual warfare. Nevertheless, every day of our lives, everyone of us is enmeshed in the battle between good and evil; between God and Satan for our soul. Satan himself, and those he directs, do everything they can to separate us from God. They also work to block our awareness that evil is real and active in our personal lives. It is surprising to find that many people do not believe that Satan is an actual force which roams this earth with the power to direct what occurs in our lives. But scripture tells us that he is, and that he will, remain active and he will increase the harm he brings to man as we move into the end times. If we understand and accept this force as dangerous **to us,** we realize the importance of recognizing and overcoming the satanic lies which inundate us. With little conversation and direction about what we must watch for and how Satan operates, Satan is free to plant thoughts in our mind which make us doubt God. These might be: "Yes, be afraid because when you suffered so much in the past, God didn't change that circumstance so why would He change this one?" or "Why would a God who loves you so much make such unreasonable demands of you?" or "God will forgive whatever you do because a loving God understands why you do it." **Therefore our lack of understanding of God's words and of Satan's work creates our entrapment. And our lack of trust in God *keeps* us trapped.** Most of us have been through difficult times; times when we have walked through a dark valley and wondered if we would emerge unscathed on the other side. Most of us know what it is like to be afraid, to wonder how we can change, or at least grow from, our very painful present circumstances. Interestingly, the 23rd Psalm speaks about a valley which we must walk through and tells us that as we leave for this journey, God is with us. As we envision a valley we might also think about the mountains which formed that valley and wonder what we would find on the other side, and how steep or dangerous the climb would be. We may search for which mountain seems to offer the easiest climb and we may also consider that when a valley is surrounded by mountains, it is vulnerable to water run-off, to mud slides, avalanches, and even the severity of the weather swirling around its highest point. Further, mountains can block the sun and cause the valley to be dark, forbidding and cold. Nevertheless we may dream of climbing that mountain and leaving the valley in an effort to change our life. We may long to make a change in our life, but not know how to do so. To provide a little analogy to this thought, let me indulge in a little tale which can explain what can occur as we search for a way out of our troubles. Here is a tale describing a child of God who is searching for answers, is given an answer and decides to follow it's advice....until she allows the fear which Satan places in her heart to stop her.

Climbing The Mountain

"Once upon a time a child of God found herself transported to the darkest valley imaginable and found that she was surrounded by a tall mountain range. She hadn't expected to find herself there and as she looked around, she could feel the lack of warmth and sunlight in these new surroundings. This brought fear to her heart. She was alone and she was afraid.

Over time, she knew that the valley was not where she wanted to be and she began to wonder why she stayed in the valley where she was so unhappy. So she looked for a way to change this circumstance. As she looked around, she saw many majestic mountain peaks surrounding the valley. She also saw a path on each of the mountains and each seemed to begin in the valley and reach the very top of the mountain. She wondered if she could find one of those paths and begin the climb to leave the valley. She also wondered which path she should try because she did not know what was on the other side of any of those mountains. So she prayed and asked God to show her the path that He wanted her to take. God heard the prayers of His child and He answered them. He summoned the sun to shine behind one of the peaks and send its light over the clouds, highlighting the blue of the skies, and allowing her see the birds flying over the path. The light revealed the path she was to take.

But as she walked across the valley and was about to step onto the pathway filled with sunlight, a storm suddenly appeared in front of her. The path ahead filled with lightning and with torrential rains. She watched the side of the path become muddy and slide away into the woods, and she saw trees split from the lightning, and she was filled with fear.

She was afraid to move forward so she turned back. She was once again confined to her valley, and in its cold, dark and lonely environment, she cried. She wondered if she would ever be free to walk again in the sunlight. She wondered if she would ever know where God wanted her to be. She wondered what it was that she was to learn from all of this. She seemed stuck in a terrible place and began to lose hope. But through it all, she continued to pray. Finally, she asked God why he'd pointed her toward a path and then made it almost impossible for her to walk that path. She asked God to help her understand why that was, and to show her what she was to do. She prayed that she could open her heart to what God wanted for her.

The child of God tried her best to listen to the little voice inside her, knowing that it was the Holy Spirit of God teaching her. One day she heard the voice ask: "Do you trust God....**really** trust Him?" She pondered this question carefully and suddenly realized that she **had fully believed** that she did trust God. However, perhaps by being afraid to take the path she had been shown, she **had not** been willing to trust after all. She was surprised by this thought because **she'd fully believed that she had trusted** God. So she prayed again and asked for forgiveness and she humbly asked God to give her another chance. The same voice that she'd heard before responded to her prayer and asked: "Why is your trust in your Heavenly Father so limited?" "Does He not have all power over everything?" "What if the lightning never struck the area where you would have walked? What if the mudslides never actually touched the path you followed? What if the trees which split fell only to the side of the path?"

And she was ashamed by those questions. She saw that God had simply wanted her to trust Him and she had **not** done so. God wanted to bring her onto a path which would lead her into the sunshine again. He wanted to show her how much He loved her and cared for her. But she had seen and rejected what God offered her. She responded only to her fear. She had not been willing to **fully** trust that God would walk beside her and protect her. So, God's child prayed yet again and asked God to open her understanding, give her courage, fill her with strength and perseverance, and to bind the forces of Satan which brought fear to her heart. And God did. And so God's child again found the path God had set before her and with trust and courage, she began to climb."

What this little story tells us is that as fear overtakes us, and what we face appears overwhelming, we often falter. We lose our courage or we lose the strength to keep going. We lose our trust! We retreat back to **what we know, what is familiar** to us. We give in to our fears and seek the comfort zone of what we were hoping to leave even though we know it was not good for us. This shows us how difficult it is to trust God _enough_ to **break from the old patterns** we have espoused. But this little story also helps us recognize that **we need help** to reach the goal of our faith. We are weak, we are sinners and **we need God's help.** John 8:44-45 warns against believing Satan's lies and not believing what God tells us: "Ye are of your father the devil.......there was no truth in him...... **he speaketh a lie**........And because I tell you the truth, **ye believe me not.**" If we truly desire to shed our Adam-like nature and we make the effort to put in the work this requires; the sweat and tears to **trust God to lead us into a Christ-like nature;** we are promised an incredible future. As we begin to understand God's plan and **trust His advice** and the promises He provides, we will come to a crossroad where we face the need to either **accept or reject** what we have learned. If we accept God's words as truth, we will never be lukewarm toward God and will make the commitment to Him

with all our heart and no longer fear. God wants our commitment to that love and to His way of life so that a people of one goal, one mind, and one heart can live in harmony for all eternity. And if we falter on the way, God will forgive us, help us to our feet again and strengthen us to try again. But we have to be willing to walk **through our fears** to follow God, ***knowing that He will not allow us to be harmed!*** Satan on the other hand wants us to fail and does not want us to try again. He will use his power to place every possible obstacle in our path and to **heighten every fear imaginable.** Our only recourse is to keep God's words in our heart and in our minds, *repeating* **God's promises over and over again to block Satan's whispers** of danger and immediate gratification. We must **fight** against the fear Satan brings and **not allow it to gain a foothold. We can do this by repeating God's promises and trusting Him.**

If we can memorize even a few of the verses where God tells us not to be afraid, to trust Him, and believe that He is always with us, we will have the ammunition to accomplish this goal. We must also list, recall and repeat the times when God helped us in the past. This will make us realize that God *always* helped us in those circumstances and usually brought a blessing from what we had to endure. 1 Peter 3:12 tells us that God's ears are open to our prayers. Isaiah 25:4 tells us that God will be a strength to the needy; a refuge. Jeremiah 33:3 says that if we call to God, He will answer. Malachi 3:10 teaches us that we can "prove" God and when we do this, He will open for us the windows of Heaven. Psalm 5:11 tells us that God will defend those who put their trust in Him. These are but a few of the myriad of promises God gives us throughout scripture. And *if we place them into our hearts and use them when we feel fearful, the spirits of fear cannot find a resting place in us.*

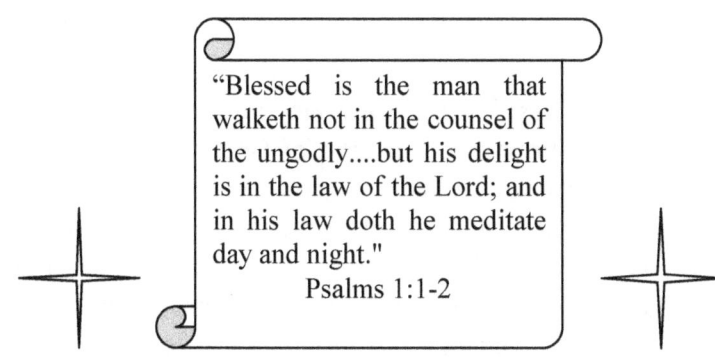

"Blessed is the man that walketh not in the counsel of the ungodly....but his delight is in the law of the Lord; and in his law doth he meditate day and night."
Psalms 1:1-2

Chapter Four

SATAN'S GOAL

Satan's anger and desperation will increase as Christ's return becomes more imminent. Satan knows that after the First Resurrection, he will have only a few years left to wreak havoc on the children of God before Christ returns for the Thousand Years of Peace. He knows that when this occurs, he and his fallen angels will be bound and placed into the Lake of Fire. Therefore, Satan's goal is to cause us to doubt that God exists by distracting us through the pain of loneliness, contention, financial burdens, relationship problems, loss or illness to delay that day. Satan wants the children of God to question why God does not step in and right the wrongs in this world. He wants us to stop believing that God will fulfill the promises we read in scripture. He wants us to wallow in our misery and blame God for our misfortune. Satan knows that most of the suffering he brings to the children of God will manifest itself in their bodies **through the emotional pain he can inflict** to our heart and mind over our circumstances. Satan knows that we are weakest emotionally and looks for the one thing in our life to which we are most vulnerable. Satan does this because he is fighting for his life. He knows that when God develops the last soul He desires for His new kingdom, Satan and his followers will be bound in the Lake of Fire. Satan believes that if he can prevent that last soul from being developed, he can remain free and delay Christ's return. To combat the incredible power Satan has in this earth and to enhance our trust in God, we must, on a daily basis, **identify the many miracles of faith which our burdens have produced *in the past.*** By examining these blessings, and seeing how many of them came out of the ashes of our sorrow, we are encouraged *not* **to focus on how our body is reacting to our current concerns.** While we may be going through some difficult times and may commiserate over how bad we feel, how fearful we are, what disappointment we are experiencing, how angry we may be, and even ask why God allowed these circumstances into our lives, in the end, we must focus on **the blessing God has *always* brought out of all of our burdens *in the past*.** This "accounting" will always lean in favor of God's response to us and it will **increase our faith, decrease our anxiety, and help us fight our current fear.**

The story of Job shows us that Job gained a new realization of his attachment to God as he endured Satan's attack and finally understood that his commitment was an everlasting one no matter what befell him. **His suffering produced an awakening in his heart and soul of his commitment to God and reinforced his belief that *no matter what happened, his love for God would not waver*** and that no matter how bad things seemed, God would bring him through. God already knew that this reaction lived in Job's heart......**but Job did not know** this at that time. (Job 5:20-27) Therefore, Job suffered his losses with grief, calamity, terror and sorrow. (Job 6:1-10) Then Job asked God to **teach him,** *cause* him to understand despite his desperate words. (Job 6:24-26) And near the end of Job's period of suffering he turned his life over to God despite his pain and said, "...*all the days of my appointed time **will I wait, till my change come.***" (Job 14:14)

Job knew that God **allowed Satan** to "***break him, take him by his neck, shake him***", (Job 16:12). What we can learn from this is that as **we** suffer and as our bodies rebel from the pain we are enduring, we are recognizing our commitment to God and proving to ourselves that with God we can endure all things. We learn that *we can speak against* those occurrences and *we can hate our circumstance* and our pain, **but despite this, we *will* remain faithful.** In Job 23:10, Job says: "*But **he (God) knoweth the way that I take:** when he hath tried me **I shall come forth as gold.***" It was at this point that God **released Job from Satan's captivity** and blessed him with double what he had before. (Job 42:10)

Job lived to be 140 years old and did so with God's blessing...<u>**not because he hadn't complained or asked questions, but because he remained faithful and acknowledged God's right to do with him as He deemed necessary to assure him of a future in God's kingdom.**</u> Therefore, whatever we suffer, however our bodies rebel against our circumstances, it is our hearts attitude, our submission, our understanding of God's plan and our love for God which will matter.

We need to trust that God **always** creates something special from the ashes of our sorrow. We need to be **willing** to learn, and to follow God's will, and then *trust that we will emerge a better person for having endured that experience.* We must be careful that we do not claim to "believe" while lacking the level of faith which God wants us to have. Many profess to "believing" in God, "believing" that Christ is the Son of God and that Christ died for us to provide a pathway for the forgiveness of our sins. But faith, ***true faith*** means that we believe *so strongly* that we fully **trust God's decisions for our lives and strive to live as God dictates because it is our learning process.** We must make the effort to subdue the Adam-like nature which makes demands on God. We must try our best to submit to what God allows into our lives. When we understand that these circumstances will bring us a lesson from which we can grow, we will have begun the process of becoming more Christ-like. Through these efforts, we will also be working to eliminate the fear which Satan brings us. But, **to understand why** Satan does what he does, we have to look back into the circumstances which made Satan, for all eternity, an outcast from God's community.

Before Satan waged war against God, Satan was the most beautiful and powerful angel in Heaven and was named Lucifer. He became jealous of Christ and later also became jealous of mankind when he discovered that God would give man a higher rank than He gave the angels. Lucifer's beauty and power were immense and gave him the means by which he could draw one third of all the angels in heaven to his goal of stopping God from fulfilling this plan. Lucifer also desired to become the ruler of heaven himself. But, in time he was thrown out of Heaven for his rebellion and was then called the Devil, Satan, Beelzebub, the Prince of darkness, the serpent, the father of lies, and many other names.

God's rule of righteousness and the free will God gave to mankind demands that **mankind choose** between the good God offers and the evil and rebellion Satan offers. Thus Satan was allowed to keep the power with which he tries to win mankind to his side. Satan's followers became the demons who work to prevent man from learning of and obeying God. They fully understand God's Plan of Salvation and what will happen to them when God's plan is complete. Satan and his fallen angels know scripture and know that if man disobeys God just as they did, man cannot reside with God. They know that God's Plan of Salvation cannot be completed until the number of souls God wants are developed. They believe that delaying the completion of God's Plan allows them to retain their power and escape punishment for their rebellion. Nevertheless, God's plan does move forward and *will* be completed. *Every* fallen angel who harmed God's children and rebelled against God will be thrown into the Lake of Fire with Satan and with the unredeemed souls of mankind who chose not to follow God's statutes. Thus Satan, his angels, and the unredeemed souls of mankind will be placed into the Lake of Fire, also known as Hell, and remain there for all eternity **forever separated from God and *continuously* tormented** by hatred, anger, envy, jealousy, back biting, cruelty, lies, slander and all things evil. It is through God's Plan of Salvation that good and evil will be separated forever. Evil will **not** be allowed to enter God's new kingdom and will be bound forever in the Lake of Fire.

All of mankind must be absolved of sin to become a part of God's new kingdom. 1 Corinthians 10:21 warns that we **cannot be partakers of the Lord .... and with devils**. 1 John 1:8 tells us that **we deceive ourselves if we think that we are without sin.** 1 Kings 8:46 and 2 Chronicles 6:36 explain that **there is no man who is without sin.** And Matthew 5:24 tells us that **no one can serve two masters**. In fact, scripture covers every detail of our spiritual life from what God deems a sin, to how we are to obtain forgiveness. It teaches us what God plans for our future and what we must do while still here on earth to be found worthy. It also teaches us that from the ranks of mankind, God will choose those who are the most faithful to become a "bride" for His Son and that this "family" will reside in the City of God. God will also choose those who are His lambs, those who will be the inhabitants who reside outside the city gates in Heaven.

But we are warned throughout scripture that out of the ranks of mankind there will also emerge a group of people who scripture calls the "goats". These people did not want to learn of God, follow God's statutes, or believe scripture. They may have harmed God's work, or harmed the children of God by ignoring God's admonition to "*love thy neighbor*". The "goats" will be placed into the Lake of Fire with Satan and his fallen angels for all eternity. As we learn these truths we see clearly that **it is up to us, it is our own free will with which we will choose our place. Our actions will determine where we will be assigned and whether we will become a part of the bride of Christ, a lamb in Heaven, or a goat.** Scripture provides us with everything we need to learn of God's plan and our place in that plan. But it will be up to us to choose to live here on earth in a manner which pleases God or in a manner which supports evil. There are only three groups into which everyone who ever lived or died or was conceived will fall into, and **it is our free will which will direct what place we will occupy for all eternity.** Satan's goal is to disrupt God's Plan of Salvation by breaking the faith of those God wants for His new Heaven and Earth. Satan knows that God has a certain number of souls He is developing, and therefore Satan targets those souls specifically. If we do not know God's Plan of Salvation or how and why Satan does what he does, it is more difficult to thwart Satan's attacks, prevent the fear he places into our hearts or the complacency which keeps us from God's words.

"I have seen his ways, and will heal him; I will lead him also, and restore comforts unto him.....Peace, peace to him....and I will heal him."

Isaiah 57:18-19

Chapter Five

LOSING WHAT WE LOVE

One of the most difficult circumstances we experience is when death takes someone we love. It can cause our emotions to undergo a bevy of ups and downs. As children of God, we may know what we must do and how we must think when we go through such a loss, but nonetheless, we struggle with the pain it brings. The spiritual part of our nature, the Christ-like nature which we strive to develop, teaches us to be thankful that our loved one remained faithful to God as their journey here on earth ended and they achieved the goal of their faith. We believe that God's timing is perfect and that it is He who chooses when each of us should leave this earth. This spiritual part of our nature helps us accept what occurred and trust God's decision. But it is our human nature (the Adam-like nature) which tries to block this aspect of our thought process. When the Adam-like nature whispers its discontent and doubt, and we feel fear and anxiety from those thoughts, we suddenly find that it is a struggle to trust that God has a plan for us; one that can still be filled with happiness. Instead, we worry about how our natural lives will change and whether or not we will handle our loss with the dignity of acceptance. We hope that over time we will fully accept God's decision because we **want** to trust God. We try to diminish our pain by accepting what God ordains, but we still must struggle with the realization that we will no longer share the daily companionship and interaction which we were once privileged to experience. For some there is the added disappointment over an injustice our loved one might have experienced or how a modern day "Pharisee" tried to diminish God's role in what occurred. But it is at this time that **we must personally decide how we will conduct ourselves;** how **we** will begin our steps on the new path God has set before us. It is at this time that we must continue to grow in our spiritual life, allow God to deal with whatever injustice, pain, activity or loss may have occurred and be satisfied with **whatever future** God ordains for us.

As we digest these changes to our life and face them each day, it is natural to feel **lonely, afraid, and confused**. We may be dismayed to suddenly realize how easy it had been to pray when we had someone to pray with and now, when we must pray alone it is so different. Nevertheless, **we must continue** to pray and accept full responsibility to do so as faithfully as we had before. Thus, **the loss we face also becomes a test of our faith and of the effort we put forth to accept what God has ordained for us.** We are thrown into the realization that our task is to *prove to ourselves* that we trust God's decisions and are thankful for the opportunity to grow in faith **in a new and different way**. We must come to terms with the changes we face even though it is an uncomfortable situation. We must realize that our adjustment can *only* occur if we strengthen our relationship with our Heavenly Father. We may even fear that without our loved one we will always be alone in life. We may fear that God has abandoned us even though our faith assures us that **we do not stand alone** because God is with us and will help us. We must open our heart to the decision God made which has affected us so deeply, and must acknowledge and trust that God always has and will continue to provide for us, strengthen us and bring us a blessing. We must turn to God's words in scripture for the comfort He offers such as is found in Joshua 1:9: *"Have I not commanded you?* ***Be strong*** *and of good courage;* ***be not dismayed****: For* ***the Lord God is with thee withersoever thou goest."***

However, we also face the enemy of our soul, Satan, who does **not** want us to trust God or be productive in the Lord's work. He wants us to wallow in the heartache of what we have lost and *lose our strength; live with fear; blame God; and lose our faith.* Therefore, we must **pray for God's help** to keep His words of comfort and direction in front of us and keep the goal of our faith in our heart by **clinging to the altar and our bearers of blessing and those God sends to help us.....and be thankful.** If this is our goal, even if we fail a number of times, we can remind our Heavenly Father of His words in 1 Corinthians 17:26-27 where we read: *"And now Lord,* ***Thou art God, And hast promised*** *this goodness unto Thy servant. Now therefore let it please Thee* ***to bless the house of Thy servant,*** *that it may be before Thee forever; for Thou blesses O Lord, and it shall be blessed forever."* God always keeps His promises.

There are many who feel that they became a better person because of the positive influence of the person they have lost. Now, with that person gone, they wonder if they can continue to strive in the manner which they did before. Since they no longer have that someone special to lean on who encouraged them and was an example to them, they must now decide, using their free will, to **prove their faith and become all that God wants them to become. Satan fully understands these challenges and knows what these fears can do.** He is aware that we are weak, that the pain of our loss makes us vulnerable. He knows that we still have much to overcome. **Satan uses our vulnerability in his attacks to break our trust and destroy our faith in God. He uses our natural fears against us and augments those fears with his whispers of a bleak future. But as children of God we know that our Heavenly Father promises to help and protect us.** God tells us that if we try, if we do our best, if we desire to grow in faith, He will be right beside us; He will guide us with His hand and **He will protect us** from that which Satan brings against us. **Therefore we have nothing to fear!**

As mentioned in an earlier chapter, to fight these fears **we must recall the many ways which God has blessed us in the past. We must be thankful** for what time we did have with our loved one. **Satan will bring to mind the pain and fear** we naturally feel in our new situation. **He does not want us to trust God. He wants us to fear the changes we face.** When we succumb to the fear Satan brings, we must remind ourselves that God has told us not only how we are to conduct ourselves during this change in our life, but will also bless us for our godly conduct. He even promises to give us the desires of our heart! God explains in Philippians 4:8 what our personal task is: *"Finally brethren, whatever things are* ***true****, whatever things are* ***noble****, whatever things are* ***just****, whatever things are* ***pure****, whatever things are* ***lovely****, whatever things are* ***of good report****, if there is any* ***virtue*** *and if there is anything* ***praiseworthy****-meditate on these things."*

We can also be comforted by remembering that **when Christ faced death on the cross for our sake,** *He also felt fear* **and prayed to His Heavenly Father to ask Him to remove** this terrible ordeal He faced. But despite His fear, Christ provided an example to each of us when He ended His conversation with His Heavenly Father with the words: *"Thy will be done"*. Christ's words help us understand that **fear is easily brought by Satan and implanted into our human state but God is aware of this,** and will help us overcome it. God wants us to *take the leap of faith to trust His decision for our lives no matter how difficult it may appear to be.* He loves us and wants us to be happy. He comforts us with the words in 1 Corinthians 2: 9: *"Eye hath not seen, nor ear heard, neither have entered into the heart of man, the things which God hath prepared for them that love Him."* And He also tells us in Revelation 3:8: *"**I know thy works**: behold, I have set before thee an open door, and no man can shut it: for thou hast a little strength, and hast kept my word, and hast not denied my name."* Knowing God's words can comfort us, and while the pain of our loss remains a palpable reality we must remember that our human nature requires **time** to adjust. *The greater our faith, the shorter the time it takes to heal.* Our prayer life, what we hear in the Divine Services, and the help and support we obtain from those who reach out to comfort us, are but some of the gifts God sends to help us. By clinging to God's ways we will bear what we have experienced.... **and one day see the blessing of God's perfect decision.** We will also obtain a blessing on our future for accepting God's will with a heart that will continue to seek God. Nevertheless, dealing with the loss of a loved one is easier said than done and God understands this. Those who have lived through this experience understand the difficulty it presents. Therefore God asks us to **comfort those who undergo the heartaches we have lived through** and wants us to know what Christ told Simon in Luke 22:32: *"But I have prayed for thee, **that thy faith fail not**; and when thou art converted, **strengthen thy brethren**."* As we heal, we can hold fast to the words in Revelations 3:11 which remind us: *"I come quickly; hold that fast which thou hast, that no man take thy crown."* And then in Revelation 7:17: *".....and **God shall wipe away all tears** from their eyes."* We must remember that God often takes us home when we have reached the peak of our spiritual growth. That is a great blessing......and is something we would never want to take away from our loved one. We must also remember that ***we will meet them again***. 1 Thessalonians 17-18 tells us: *"...the dead in Christ shall rise first. Then **we who are alive...shall be caught up together with them**......"*

To thwart Satan's plan to break our faith through fear, Ephesians 6:11-12 teaches: *"Put on the **whole** armour of God, that ye may be able to **stand against the wiles of the devil**. For **we wrestle not against flesh and blood but against principalities, against powers, against the rulers of the darkness of this world, against spiritual wickedness in high places**."* Luke 11:20-22 teaches that God is more powerful than Satan. God's Apostles were given the power to cast these devils out of man and to teach us **what** we must watch for so that we will not succumb to these evil powers. Luke 24-26 warns that the spirits which bring us such pain can **re-enter man** if he does not repent of his sin. These spirits can fill our soul with ungodly endeavors, false doctrines, and activities which force the Holy Spirit to leave. There are many who, just like the Pharisees, pray in public, yet harm their neighbor, never making restitution for their wrong-doing. Others seek ways to refute scripture and lean toward their own understanding. They will lose their soul salvation because they have allowed arrogance and evil to guide them. Scripture, God's direct instruction to mankind, provides us with every nuance of His Plan of Salvation and explains how Satan works to prevent that plan from being completed. Scripture teaches us to look *inward* so we can spurn satanic attacks and understand why it is necessary to learn God's words to do so. As God's words unfold and we recognize the qualities required in those God wants for His kingdom, we realize that we **must change**. We must adjust our thoughts and actions to accommodate God's words, shed our old nature and shed our arrogant know-it all attitude. We must become more loving, giving and understanding. We must take on the Christ-like nature God longs for in all His children. **We must trust God's decisions** for our life. But *if we don't learn God's words, we won't recognize the work of Satan and his followers*, nor understand that Satan's followers can unleash such great fear and anxiety in our hearts that we no longer trust God.

The Holy Spirit also offers to help us by unveiling the mysteries of scripture and enhancing our understanding of God's words. **When the Holy Spirit can abide in us, we will learn and overcome more rapidly.** 1 Peter 5:8 warns: *"Be sober, be vigilant, because your **adversary the devil,** as a roaring lion, walketh about, seeking who he may devour."* Mark 13:20 says: *"And except that the Lord hath shortened, those days, **no flesh should be saved**; but for the elect's sake, whom he hath chosen, he hath shortened them."* God wants us to value His ways and trust Him. He wants us to have full access to the power which the sacrifice of Christ affords us. (John 14:23) Colossians 1:13 tells us that the triumph of Christ *"....hath **delivered us from the power of darkness,** and hath translated us into the kingdom of His dear Son."* Christ could have overpowered the evil forces which brought Him to those who crucified Him, but Romans 13:1-7 explains that God allowed those satanic forces to exercise their power not only to bring mankind forgiveness, but also **to fulfill the words of scripture, execute the prophecies foretelling the sacrifice of Christ and, in righteousness, separate good from**

evil for all eternity. As we learn, we are strengthened and we begin to trust that God ultimately controls everything. We realize that God **purposely** gave authority to evil so that through righteousness, good can be separated from evil for all eternity. God *allows* **satanic activity for the development of man's soul.** Man must **use** his free will to decide **who** he will follow, God or Satan. Therefore **mankind must choose God and His ways of righteousness and spurn what Satan offers and** *make that choice of his own free will.*

Mankind's original fall to Satan gave Satan "custody" of us. God's righteousness had to allow Satan to claim the "rights" he'd earned when man sinned. Sin demands that a ransom be paid for our souls but Christ paid that ransom by sacrificing His life, a sinless life, to satisfy that claim and offer us freedom. For us to claim that freedom, we must take what God has offered and what Christ has done for us and through a repentant heart, utilize the sacrament of Holy Communion to be free. This helps us overcome Satan's power and helps us prove our faith. God promises to help us and He teaches us everything we need to learn through His words in scripture. God promises in Luke 24:45 to open our understanding of the scriptures so we can learn from them. And in Matthew 5:6 He promises to bless those who hunger after righteousness. Revelation 21:4 tells us that God promises to wipe away all the tears, death and sorrow attached to our struggle here on earth. Revelation 2:26 tells us that whoever will keep God's words *and do His works* will be given a crown.

Fear is Satan's greatest weapon against us. Thus Proverbs 29:25 teaches: *"The fear of man bringeth a snare, but whoso putteth his trust in the Lord shall be safe."*

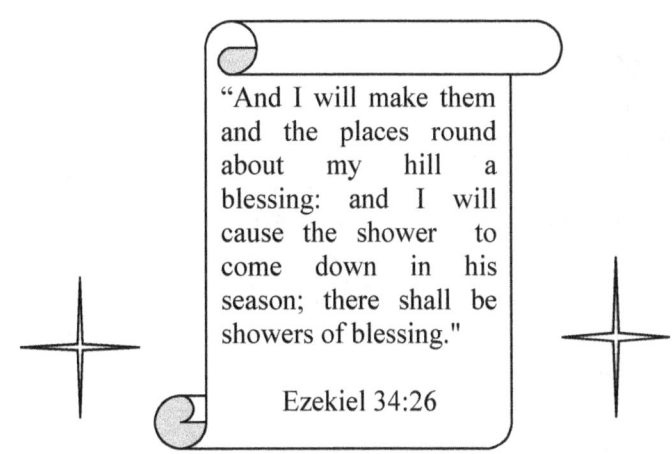

"And I will make them and the places round about my hill a blessing: and I will cause the shower to come down in his season; there shall be showers of blessing."

Ezekiel 34:26

Chapter Six

HOW DO I LEARN TO TRUST GOD?

In order to trust God, we have to know Him. In order to know Him, we must understand what God has done for us, will do for us, and why. To do this, we have to start at the beginning when God created this world and began with the heavens and the waters and all in His Creation which would impact mankind. God completed the Creation by creating man and the miracle of developing the souls with whom He would share His future kingdom. It is through the Creation that we learn what lives in God's heart and what future He wishes to provide for us. **All He did, He did for us** and everything which He created, He saw as good. (Genesis 1:10) When all was in place, Genesis 1:31 tells us that God considered what He had done to be *"very good"*! These two words tell us that what God created contained no evil and no sin...it was perfect, it was *beautiful and beneficial and diverse.* The Creation also gives us great insight into God's power, His artistic abilities, and the beauty and generosity of His heart.

God created everything for a purpose and works toward seeing that purpose fulfilled. Thus everything God created worked together in harmony, and was equally blessed. But when sin entered the heart of Adam and Eve through Satan, the blessing was lost and a curse came upon the Creation. When Satan could finally exercise his power over mankind through the disobedience of Adam and Eve, many other aspects of the Creation also fell into disharmony including everyone who was yet to be born or conceived. What had once been perfect became imperfect under the curse of sin, and the entire earth, including mankind, lost the blessing they'd once enjoyed.

Just as Satan entered God's Creation to interject misunderstanding, disobedience, and disharmony so has he entered man's heart today to fill Him with pride, arrogance, self-satisfaction, envy, hatred, and sin, along with a sense of entitlement and self-righteousness. Satan perverts our thoughts in an effort to destroy our understanding that God loves us, God sees our potential, and wants us to develop into those who will spend an eternity with Him even while **He hates our sin**. Despite our faults and failings, God works to teach us how to overcome the Adam-like nature which allows fear, envy and disobedience to govern us and cause us to harm ourselves and others. God wants us to learn His ways so we can turn to the Christ-like nature which fights sin and thwarts sin. God gave us our free will so **we can decide which** attitude and which nature we want to embrace. Free will allows *us* to choose between righteousness which makes us thankful, loving, trusting and sin-free *or* unrighteousness which encourages us to be angry, hateful, fearful and sinful. **Free will forces us to take responsibility for our choices; for what those choices bring into our lives, and what they ultimately mean to God and our soul salvation. We can only learn however, by learning what God tells us through**

scripture. Scripture teaches us to look for the "beam" in our own eye rather than the "speck" in our brother's eye....and to have the knowledge about how to pluck it out. Fear is one of these beams. God encourages us to **choose** to trust Him rather than succumb to the fear which ultimately produces the lethargy which inhibits us from correcting the harmful patterns we repeat. Satan espouses hate, anxiety, anger, fear, gossip and lies and is always cunning, sly, plotting, malicious, jealous and unappreciative. Evil makes us proud and haughty, self-serving and unloving. Evil creates justification for sin, and for self importance. The pursuit of righteousness makes us happy and honest, open and supportive, appreciative and humble, giving and loving. Righteousness removes fear and replaces it with peace. Righteousness helps us to esteem others higher than ourselves.

God asks us to *appreciate where He placed us and* in that place *work toward perfecting the heart and soul we have been given.* God gave us the talents we have because He would like us to use them to draw souls to Him. He wants us to **develop** what He gave us and become the best we can. Through God, **through our appreciative heart** *and the acknowledgement and forgiveness of sin,* we do find righteousness and joy.... and satisfaction.... no matter what circumstance we find ourselves in. Under God's care we can grow strong in whatever place or circumstance we find ourselves.....*if* **we know what God tells us and try to incorporate His directives into our lives. Happiness is not tied to material possessions, beauty, talent, or the temporal, but tied only to the heart and the amount and purity of the love it holds and attitudes it espouses.** Let us not allow the whispers of Satan to weaken us or cause us to live *in fear.* Let God help us grow in strength and trust so we can become those who seek to learn what we can "do" to make this happen; what we can put into place in our lives to help us reduce our sin and increase our trust in God.

Scripture makes many references to the lambs of God, to His flock, to the Shepherd who looks after the lambs. It also refers to the need to "feed" the sheep. As we ponder these words and think about the many references to sheep which we find in scripture, we begin to recognize its importance. Therefore it is crucial that we study these words, and try to understand how sheep and their shepherd might apply to **our** lives. Scripture also makes many references to the fear we carry in our hearts and tells us over and over again **not** to fear. In fact, we see these words so often throughout scripture that **these too should be pondered.** Therefore we need to learn what fear is, where it comes from, why we suffer from it, and what we are to do about it. We need to learn about sheep and shepherds. Interestingly, when we consider these words together, we are reminded of the 23rd Psalm where God tells us that the Lord is our Shepherd and that **we should not fear** evil. As we read these 118 words in the King James Bible, we can note that the verbs used in this Psalm indicate the here and now, not the past. They clearly tell us that the Lord **"is"** my shepherd.... not that He was, or will be, but **is**...right now! We also know that sheep are followers. They rely on their shepherd to bring them to a viable pasture where they can find the nourishment they require. Sheep also rely on their shepherd to find safe and suitable water for them to drink, and to guard them from predators. They are docile in nature and after they have eaten, they lie down in the pasture to bring up again or "ruminate" what they ate; that which the shepherd provided for them. These activities give us extraordinary insight into what God wants **us to know and apply** to our life. They provide us with an incredibly eye opening lesson about how we must **listen** to God's words,

think about them, **digest** them, and **trust** the Shepherd of our soul to provide what we need, and protect us.

Hundreds of thousands of people suffer from fear; some from post traumatic stress syndrome, some from panic attacks, some from sudden unbidden glimpses into an unhappy past, some from the sins they have committed, and others from the sins committed against them. Many take medication to help them deal with this fear, yet few ask why this fear has such power over them. Nor do they ask what advice God gives us about the spirit of fear. Scripture does tell us that fear is placed into our heart by an evil spirit and that **it is not God who brings us fear nor does He want us to feel fear.** In fact, **God wants us to overcome the spirit of fear and will help us do so.** But, as in combating all evil, we can only be helped when we have reached the point in our faith where we have acknowledged, and repented of, our sins. When we desire to make restitution to those we harmed; when we have forgiven those who sinned against us; when we have **learned Gods words** enough to apply them; and when we have asked God to help us, **and are *willing* to trust Him, He will help.** God's righteousness works best when we take these steps. They allow Him to work all of His miracles in our soul. When we have sincerely made this effort, God will step in with power and might, and **the spirit of fear will no longer have fertile ground** in our hearts **and will leave.**

The 23rd Psalm is found in the very middle of the Bible and speaks of **today**. Interestingly, the 22nd Psalm speaks of yesterday and the 24th Psalm speaks of tomorrow, but the 23rd Psalm is for us, **for today**, for what God is offering us right now. It begins with the words *"The Lord is my shepherd"*. We can see that "is" and "my" are the keywords in this sentence. This Psalm then tells us: *"He* *restoreth my soul"*. "Restoreth" means that we have lost something which God wants to return to us. Then we read the words: *"I **will** fear no evil: for thou art with me"*. The word "will" tells us that from this point on we **"will"** not fear. The words **"with me"** tells us that we now realize that God is not some far away entity who is unaware of our circumstances, but that He **"is" "with" "us"** right this minute through whatever we are going through. Reading further into this psalm we read: *"Thou preparest a table....in the presence of mine enemies"*. The word "thou" shows us that God Himself is going to nourish us, and *"mine enemies"* tells us that no matter how close the danger (or pain or fear) appears to be, these cannot approach the places where God Himself lives; therefore it cannot harm those God protects. These words are incredibly powerful and have deep meaning for each of us. Interestingly, after sheep eat, they lie down in the pasture and while relaxing in this manner, they bring the food they recently ate back up to chew again before it enters into their system as nourishment. This process is called "ruminating" and though it applies to sheep, it clearly describes what the children of God should do with God's words. This explains that we should draw God's words into our bodies through our ears. Then we should relax and bring those words back to our thoughts and then "chew" them so that we can properly and more fully digest them thereby nourishing our body, mind and soul with them. This is beneficial advice because when we truly **digest God's words by first hearing them, then thinking about them, then pushing them into every part of our being,** we will always feel God's presence and will remember His directives and promises. Even though Satan **has** won the right to invade our souls as a result of sin, God can stop him from harming us if we use the word of God to protect ourselves. When Adam and Eve sinned and when our ancestors sinned, and then when we sinned, Satan gained access to the soul through what scripture calls inherited sin. Thus the spirit of fear (and many other spirits) could enter man not only because of his own sin, but also through the sins committed by others. The only protection we have is to "put on" the "armour" which God provides through His word and sacraments. The sacraments do however have certain prerequisites for using them as a resource to further access God's protection. Sadly, many are not aware of these pre-requisites even though they are found in scripture. One is that we **learn** God's words and apply them to our lives. Our ignorance of these matters keep us under the rule of Satan. Another is that we **work** to rid ourselves of the evil spirits and what they bring us. Another is that we **partake** of the sacraments of Baptism, Holy Communion, and Holy Sealing. It is only through the **worthy** application of Holy Communion that we can be free of the sin which keeps us bound. Further, scripture tells us that taking Holy Communion **unworthily** can bring us spiritual harm. 1 Corinthians 11:27 says: *"Wherefore **whosoever shall eat** this bread and drink this cup of the Lord, **unworthily**, shall be guilty of the body and blood of the Lord."* This reminds us that **we must acknowledge our sin, have remorse for it, *desire* not to commit it again and forgive others if we want to participate in this sacrament worthily**. Without understanding Satan's claim on us, nor the righteousness under which God chooses to act, nor how to participate in Holy Communion worthily, we remain in fear, remain in sin, and **must re-visit the same difficulties over and over again**. But when we learn what we must do and then do it, we *will* receive the fullness of God's blessing and experience the miracle which offers us freedom from these spirits.

The 9th verse of the 24th Psalm tells us: *"Lift up your heads, O ye gates; even lift them up, ye everlasting doors; and **the King of glory shall come in.**"* Any sin will cause us to walk with our head down and cause us to be blinded to **spiritual truth.** This verse also tells us that until we lift our heads up through the forgiveness of our sin, through the new purity of our heart, through the honor and integrity and love God wants us to develop, we cannot cause the gates of Satan's captivity to open and we cannot open the door to God's heart. Without learning God's words and promises, and *longing* to be obedient to His words, we do not open our hearts to God so that He can help us. The 23rd Psalm closes with the words, *"....goodness and mercy shall follow me all the days of my life: and I will dwell in the house of the Lord for ever."* This is **an incredible promise......for today!** The minute we make the decision to belong to God and do our best to learn what He wants us to know, we will receive God's help. When we **yearn** strongly enough to change our lives, **desire** not to re-visit the same difficulties over and over again, and **keep** God's words and promises in our hearts and heads, we will **banish the fear** which can so easily destroy us.

Isaiah 40:12 pointedly asks: *"**Who** measured the waters....weighed the hills?"* Job 38:8 asks: *"**Who** shut up the sea with doors?"* Job 38:35 asks: *"Can thou send lightnings?"* and Revelations 7:1 addresses who commands the angels who hold back the four winds of the earth. All of these verses and many more make us aware of our universe and the power behind it. Through scripture we learn of the might of God and all that He has done and will do for His children. We are reminded that an incredible God of power and strength **loves us and wants to help us.** Sin allows fear to damage our faith, damage our bodies, cause illness and certainly cause continuous anxiety. But scripture tells us that if we cling to the altar of grace and receive Holy Communion worthily, we need not be afraid because God will be with us wherever we go (Joshua 1:9). And Roman's 8:31 asks: *"If God be for us, who can be against us?"*

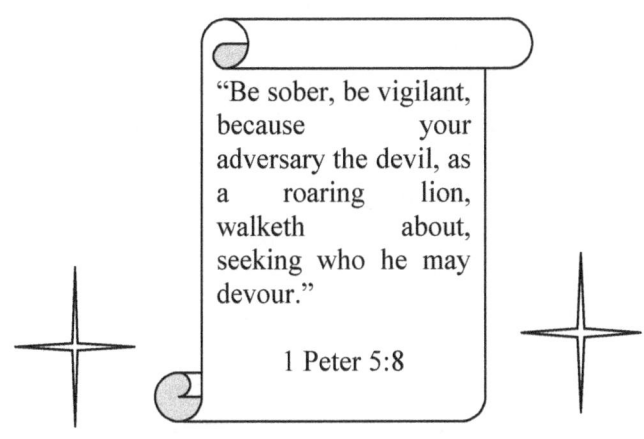

"Be sober, be vigilant, because your adversary the devil, as a roaring lion, walketh about, seeking who he may devour."

1 Peter 5:8

Chapter Seven

JUST SAY "NO"!

Usually we can discover why we suffer physical pain and find a way to treat it. But emotional pain can defy description, be harder to understand, and be more difficult to bear than physical pain. Fear is an emotion which can cause some of the worst reactions we have ever experienced. It's pain can be debilitating. When fear is activated, it penetrates deep inside our brain where it will remain, sending its tentacles to every part of our body; waiting to be activated again whenever we encounter the stimuli from which it was born. It is therefore, very difficult to erase. When our bodies react to something which causes us even momentary fear, all of our negative past experiences rise to the forefront enhancing the fear we feel at that moment. Thus we are thrust **back into the same pattern** of debilitating emotion over and over again. But since Romans 8:28 tells us: *"All things work together for the good of those that love the*

Lord", we are to trust that **our Heavenly Father wants to turn our heartache into a blessing and turn our fear into a trust so great that** <u>we can fight the fear which Satan brought us</u>. The knowledge that God promises to fix our problem, and our remembrance of the blessings God has already bestowed upon us helps us in this fight. We must use our **past blessings** to **re-program** our initial re-action to the fear stimuli.

The life we live here on Earth is the training ground from which we grow into the children of God. **How we handle our circumstances is a marker for the development of our character.** Our pain is often so great however that we wonder **how this promise of good brought out of pain could be possible.** We don't want to believe that pain might be what **we need** to develop spiritually. We find it difficult to admit that **we may require** the lessons we currently endure to make us listen. Further, when we fail to overcome our fear, Satan uses that failure to make us think that we will *never* learn and will *always* be undergoing the pain we are currently experiencing. Satan wants us to feel guilty and hopeless. He wants our debilitating emotions to cause us to give up trying to please God or believing that God loves us despite our failures. **He does not want us to believe God will help us.**

As mentioned in an earlier chapter, scripture provides us with a beautiful example of feeling fear and struggling through that fear to do God's will. It is found in Christ's reaction to what He had to face on the cross. Just before Christ was to be arrested and then crucified, He prayed, asking His Father to *"Take away this cup from me"*. This indicates that Christ feared what He would go through and wanted God to remove the need for Him to undergo that circumstance. But, the love in Christ's heart and **the trust He had in His Father allowed Him to submit to His** circumstances and to bring forth the noble character in His soul..... **despite His fear.** Christ completed His prayer saying: *"**Nevertheless, not what I will, but <u>what thou will</u>"***. These words tell us that God allows us to express our fear and wish our circumstances were different. They also tell us that we are **not judged and found lacking to ask God to take our troubles away.** But it also teaches us that if we tell Him that we know that <u>**His will, not ours**</u> is best for us and is therefore what we **want** in our lives, we then prove our character. When we adjust our thoughts and actions to submit to God's will, Satan realizes that he **cannot** break our trust in God, and there is no further reason for him to continue his harassment. **When this occurs, we are often released from Satan's captivity and thus released from our fear.** The key words here however are: *we accept God's will* for us".

As we examine Christ's words of submission, we appreciate His sacrifice even more. We read in Mark 14:34 of how the **emotional** pain of His ordeal caused great suffering to Christ: *"My soul is **exceedingly sorrowful** unto death."* Christ prayed: *"Abba Father, all things are possible unto thee. **Take away this cup from me,** nevertheless **not what I will** but **what thou will.**"* Christ later **repeated** this plea a **second time and a third time**! Therefore, when **we** are caught up in a circumstance which seems to have no end, we need not feel guilty to ask God to let our circumstances pass..... as long as our heart truly desires that God's will be paramount. It is the **trust** we place in God's design for our lives that will allow us to accept what comes and to ***not fear it!*** **Our lack of fear honors God and honoring God is one of the ways we worship Him.** *Doing* God's will is also how we honor God.

John 4:23 tells us: *"But the hour is coming, and now is, when the true worshippers will worship the Father in spirit and truth; for **the Father is seeking such** to worship Him."*

This clearly tells us that God is seeking souls who will **look** for His truths, His words, **and follow** them as best they can. God knows the power Satan has over us and He knows how **fear can harm us and invade every part of our being.** This is why God provides three hundred and sixty five verses in scripture...one for every day....which make reference to **not** being afraid and **trusting God** to look after us.

As we read Christ's request to His Father we recognize that He was afraid of what was to come. But after His prayer and His subsequent submission to His Father's will, God comforted Him and gave Him the strength to complete His commission. Obviously Christ dreaded what He was to live through and felt that He had no earthly support, no true and loyal friend who would pray with Him. Nevertheless He **trusted and obeyed what His Heavenly Father ordained** *despite* **the fear and sorrow Satan brought to His heart.**

What this teaches us is that **fear is very powerful.** Fear can interfere with God's plans for us. **Fear is one of Satan's favorite tools.** Nevertheless, our spiritual growth depends on our **acceptance** of God's will for our lives, the amount of **trust** we place into accepting His will, and the effort we make to learn and **actually do** as God asks. Therefore, when Satan rears his ugly head and fills our heart with fear, we must simply say "NO"! When we say "NO" out loud, we cannot entertain the thoughts Satan wants to place in our heads. In fact, and perhaps in slightly different words, this is what Christ did when he used the words **"Get thee behind me Satan"** as recorded in Matthew 16:23.

God is pleased when we make the effort to fight our fear. God wants to give us everything..... every joy possible....and take away all fear.... but **He knows what we need to mature spiritually.** When we try to learn and finally understand His ways and accept His will for our lives, **He will create a blessing from our experiences** and we will gain not only godly wisdom, but also the ability to thwart what Satan tries to do to us. There is no doubt that **Satan's power is far greater than our own.** 1 Chronicles 21:1 tells us that Satan can *move men to do his bidding;* 1 Thessalonians 2:18 tells us that he *can hinder people*; Isaiah 14:12 explains the he *weakened nations;* 2 Corinthians 4:4 says that he can *blind the minds of non-believers;* 2 Thessalonians 2:9 warns that he can *produce signs and wonders.* There are **many** verses which tell us about the power that Satan and his fallen angels have. But God has **more** power, and it will be God's will and the completion of His Plan of Salvation which will be the winner in the end. Sometimes however, we do not want to say "NO" to Satan. Sometimes we flirt with danger because of the comfort we find in our sins and the arrogance of wanting to "know better" than scripture. Perhaps we wonder if Satan will stop his attack if we stop seeking God. Perhaps we have never explored what scripture tells us or we are complacent about its admonitions. Perhaps we think that just reaching out *a bit* to see what will happen if we dabble in sin will be okay. God knows our thought process and therefore allows us to make the mistakes which will teach us something of spiritual value. When we find ourselves in trouble and wish we had said "NO", our Heavenly Father knows that if we remain where we are for a while; remain mired in the pain we brought on ourselves; our lesson makes a greater impression on us and we may act with more caution in the future. God does not deny us these forays into the unknown but He does warn us through scripture to watch for the satanic ploys which can bring us harm. It is very easy for the spirits of this world, the fallen angels who work to harm the children of God under the direction of Satan, to enter man and dwell there making it difficult to rid themselves of their influence. **Drug or alcohol addiction is an excellent example of this type of spiritual invasion.**

Therefore God, through scripture warns us of the dangers of stepping off the pathway which He has laid out for us. God also offers the Holy Spirit to guide us away from spiritual danger and to comfort us during the attacks. But again, the Holy Spirit cannot remain in a heart full of the evil spirits of this world and will leave. Without the Holy Spirit, man becomes more susceptible than ever to these satanic spirits and can easily lose their faith. Thus, Revelation 2:7, 22 and 29, and Revelation 3:13 and 22; and Revelation 22:17 all admonish us to **listen to God's words; to really "hear" them** so that we can learn how to obtain the protection God offers us. God does not provide these words to us for **no** reason. He knows the danger and He wants to help us avoid that danger. But it is our free will with which *we must choose between what God tells us and what Satan whispers to us.*

We can remain in safety under God's protection and the Holy Spirits direction if we just say "NO" to the spirits of this world. But we cannot understand how and why these spirits work unless we know God's words, believe them, understand His Plan of Salvation, and *choose* to stay on the path God asks us to take. God's blessing is valuable and will carry us through every danger if we adhere to His words. We must learn what God considers sin, and how Satan works through that sin. God wants us to succeed and wants to protect us. Our goal is to be found worthy on the day of the First Resurrection and to do this, we must learn how and when and why to say "No" to the spirits of this world.

Revelation 20:6 promises us: *"Blessed and holy is he who has part in the First Resurrection."*

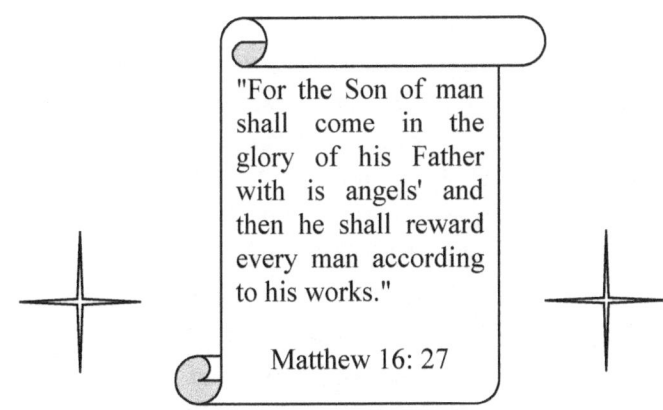

"For the Son of man shall come in the glory of his Father with is angels' and then he shall reward every man according to his works."

Matthew 16: 27

Chapter Eight

PATIENCE

Sometimes time itself can be our enemy. We live in a fast paced world where whatever we want to know is instantly available and whatever we want to buy is only a credit card away. Fast cars, highways, airports and airplanes. help us go wherever we want. Communicating with loved ones is quickly accomplished through cell phones, email and Skype. But learning to become a child of God takes time. Few of us learn quickly and most of us must make a number of mistakes before we get it right. While we know that God has allotted a certain amount of time for the Bride of Christ to "make herself ready", as we are told in Revelation 19:7, it can seem forever for those who are struggling to overcome the spirits of this world which work day and night to break their faith and hinder their progress. A true commitment to God takes time to establish and requires that we acknowledge our shortcomings and work on the areas of our life where we have failed to learn and do what God asks of us.

Because of our pride, we find it difficult to admit to our faults and failings. It isn't easy to admit that we have fallen short in our spiritual life, or have harmed God's work or His children in one way or another, or have been too lazy or busy to learn and apply His words. Nevertheless, God loves us and will forgive us when we come to Him with a humble and contrite heart. A great example of how we can be unaware of our mistakes is to examine how the blinders worn by horses who must navigate traffic laden city streets actually work. Blinders are rectangular objects designed to prevent the horse from using his peripheral vision. They are strapped onto the horses head so that what he sees is limited to what is directly in front of him. They prevent the horse from seeing anything which is on either side of him and thereby "blinds" him from those things which might distract him. This prevents the horse from reacting to a perceived danger from automobiles or other objects which suddenly appear alongside.

Satan works to place blinders on *our* eyes. He does not want us to see our errors. Thus many of us are wearing the **spiritual blinders** he places over our eyes which cause us to ignore our lack of knowledge about God and prevent us from recognizing our spiritual failings. These spiritual blinders make us **aggrandize the little good we do and the little knowledge we have about God's Plan of Salvation, while blinding us to the harm we fall under spiritually.** Scripture teaches us that making an unkind statement about someone should be counted as murder because the attitude in the heart when one does this is to "annihilate" another through that gossip. God also tells us that those who harm His children will one day wish they'd had a stone tied around their neck and they'd drowned rather than face what God will say of them when they are judged. (Matthew 18:6) But if we do not understand the gravity of committing these sins, we sin with no remorse and no change in our actions. Therefore to make changes and grow spiritually, we must remove the blinders from our eyes so that we can see the **entire** picture of **who** we are, and **how** we think, and **what** we do. **We must learn what God considers a sin** and when to flee or admonish a sinful situation. We are to come to God acknowledging each sin we have committed and ask His help to acknowledge and correct what we have not recognized. We need to work to overcome our sins and have remorse for them. Scripture teaches us that we must ask for forgiveness not only from God but also from those to whom we may have brought harm. We must try to undo the wrong we have done and do our best to "*go and sin no more*".

Sadly, **arrogance, pride and self-righteousness are powerful spirits which invade many souls and make it almost impossible for them to learn and to humble themselves in this manner**. Such souls may seek to embrace a church or religion which does **not** make the demands of spiritual change on them and will allow them to make excuses for their behavior. Many people believe that they "***have the right***" to do what they do. Yet God tells us that this is wrong. God explains that the attitude of the heart toward God, His work, and His children, is very important to our soul salvation and that the works we do are equally important. This requires that we know what scripture tells us.

Introspection is difficult and identifying and remedying what is displeasing to God in one's life takes determination, commitment and patience. Thus many die in sin. They have not, and cannot, and perhaps will not, learn God's words. Thus they do not acknowledge that they have been displeasing to God. Nor do they realize or admit that God, under His rules of righteousness ***cannot*** therefore allow them entry into His kingdom. To accept these truths would cause them to admit to the repercussions they might face because of their actions or inactions. Thus **Satan "blinds the minds of men" to these realities, preventing them from knowing what God asks of them.** However, God is not looking for perfect souls, but is looking for those who love Him; those who are contrite when they have displeased Him and those who seek to make adjustments to their lives. God is always willing to forgive us, but He looks for the humble, contrite heart which will lower its pride, leave its arrogant ways and *seek God's words and ways*. God's new kingdom will be filled with the righteous, and will contain no evil whatsoever. Sadly, few accept these "rules" for God's new kingdom. Thus scripture uses what was once thought to be an allegorical figure of only 144,000 people who will fulfill the pre-requisites to become the Bride of Christ. These will be those who sought to learn of God, and did their best to follow God's rules. In years past it was thought that this was an allegorical figure, but as we now see churches closing, Christianity attacked worldwide, see governments spurning God's existence, and see the self-serving nature of the people and their leaders, we must consider that perhaps this is an actual number after all.

Change takes time and therefore it takes patience. For every two steps ahead we take, Satan will work to make us take three steps backward. But the children of God have set their sights on the greater goal. They do not live for what this earth will bring them. They do not live for today's temporal rewards. Instead they live for a spiritual reward; an eternal future with God, with Christ as the Bridegroom of their soul, where they will be free of all sorrow, all tears, all sin and all evil. To accomplish this, God tells us to surround ourselves with believers, to go where we will hear His words, learn, and be admonished to pray, to tithe, to do our best to love others, to have remorse when we make mistakes, to rebuke one another toward righteousness, and to put on the armour of God so we can hold fast when Satan attacks.

Scripture teaches us that the "armour" which God refers to is the "taking on" or "wearing of" His words. If we know His words and His Plan of Salvation, and commit to these by bringing them "into" our way of life, God will consider us His children and always protect us. Ephesians 6:10 tells us: *"Finally, be strong in the Lord and in the strength of his power.* **Put on the whole armor of God, so that you may be able to stand against the wiles of the devil.** *For our struggle is not against enemies of blood and flesh, but against the rulers, against the authorities, against the cosmic powers of this present darkness, against the spiritual forces of evil in the heavenly places. Therefore* **take up the whole armor of God, so that you may be able to withstand on that evil day,** *and having done everything, to stand firm"*

And Ephesians 6:17 says: *"Take the helmet of Salvation and the sword of the Spirit which is* **the word of God.**"

While scripture is for everyone, God's words are specifically addressed to those who seek Him; those who **desire** to learn of Him and be a part of His Kingdom. They are for those who **hunger for righteousness** and a kinder, gentler world. They are for the souls who have a **loving heart and a passion for justice and all things good.** God in fact, tells us in Philippians 4:8 to *seek whatever is noble, just, pure, lovely, of good report, praiseworthy.* This gives us a glimpse into what God is preparing for those He loves, those who love Him enough to work toward conquering their Adam-like nature for a Christ-like nature. This does not happen overnight but takes time and effort ....and patience! Satan is patient and slowly creates difficulties for the child of God so he can strike when they are most vulnerable.

Interestingly, scripture not only tells us that we fight **"spiritual forces of evil"** but also clearly addresses and warns us about an actual **spiritual invasion**. Scripture provides many stories about how the early Apostles, and Christ Himself, cast evil spirits out of men and tells us how those spirits affected those men. Each story indicates that these spirits have the power to cause man to behave, react or act in ways which bring them harm and perhaps harm others. Moreover, Luke 11:24 and 26 quite adamantly warn that **those spirits can come back** after being cast out and can come back **seven times stronger** than before. *"When the unclean spirit is gone out of a man, he (the spirit) walketh through dry places, seeking rest; and finding none, he* (the spirit) *saith, I will return unto my house whence I came out.* ***Then goeth he, and taketh to him*** (the man) *seven other spirits more wicked than himself; and they enter in, and dwell there; and the last state of that man is worse than the first."* This gives us food for thought regarding the work of these spirits and **provides insight into the progressive nature of anxiety.**

Another example of the many evil spirits which can abide in man is found in Mark 5:1-15 which tells us in essence: *".......met...a man...with an unclean spirit....crying and cutting himself with stones....*(Christ said) ***Come out of the man, thou unclean spirit****, and asked What is thy name? And* (the unclean spirit) *answered saying, My name is Legion, for* **we are many**.....*and the unclean spirits went out....and they* (the people) *could see him that* **was possessed with the devil***, and had the legion, sitting and clothed, and in his right mind."*

Mark 1:23-27 tells us: *"And there was in their synagogue a man with an unclean spirit saying....let us alone, I know who thou art....and Jesus rebuked him saying....****come*** *out of him...and with a loud voice, he came out of him....And they were all amazed."* Another story which we find in Mark 9:19-26 tells us that a man brought his son to Jesus explaining that his son appeared to have an unclean spirit in him which made him gnash his teeth, appear depressed, and could throw him into fire or water in an effort to destroy him. That spirit also made him deaf and dumb and caused him to foam at the mouth. *"Jesus said unto him,* **if thou canst believe, all things are possible***.....and the father cried...with tears, Lord I believe, help thou my unbelief....Jesus rebuked the foul spirit saying....I charge thee,* **come out of him***.....and the spirit cried...and came out of him.....Jesus took him by the hand, and lifted him up and he arose.* And, Luke 8:2 tells us *"And certain women, which* **had been healed of evil spirits** *and infirmities, Mary called Magdalene, out of who went* **seven devils***...."*

These verses tell us that it is very possible for one or more evil spirit to enter us and exert enough influence on us to actually guide our thoughts and actions. We must consider this carefully and learn how we can **prevent this** from occurring and how we can make those spirits leave. Scripture tells us that if we are "right" with God, that the Holy Spirit will live in us, protect us and not allow any evil spirit to enter us. **Starving the evil spirit of what it needs to survive....such as our anxiety and expression of fear....will cause it to leave us and find a place where it *will* be "fed" what it desires.** Another example would be a drug addict who stops taking drugs when that spirit is no longer "fed" and it therefore must leave.

Scripture also teaches us about the trinity of God; that God is The Father, The Son and The Holy Spirit; and that The Holy Spirit was sent to man to guide and comfort him when Christ ascended into heaven. Psalm 91 is a wonderful passage for those who experience fear and anxiety and tells us: *"He is my refuge...my fortress....**shall deliver thee from the snare....Thou shall not be afraid....there shall be no evil befall thee...for he shall give his angels charge over thee.....*" And Deuteronomy 33:12 tells us: *"....The beloved of the Lord shall dwell **in safety** by him......"*   John 14:26-27 speaks directly about the Holy Spirit explaining: *"But **the Comforter**, which is **the Holy Ghost**, whom the Father will send in my name, he **shall teach you** all things, and **bring** all things **to your remembrance**, whatsoever I have said unto you. Peace I leave with you, my peace I give unto you......**let not your heart be troubled, neither let it be afraid**."* Further in John 17:15 we can read that Jesus asked His Father: *"I pray not that thou shouldst take them out of the world, but that thou shouldest **keep them from evil**."* And the Apostle Peter said in Acts 2:38: *"....Repent, and be baptised every one of you in the name of Jesus Christ for the remission of sins, and **ye shall receive the gift of the Holy Ghost.**"*

What all these verses teach us is that we need to be aware of the dangers we face in this world. We need to be aware that Satan and his fallen angels have the power and desire to bring us harm; that they **will and can** do whatever will stop us from learning about and trusting God. We also need to know that the Holy Spirit is available to us to protect us and teach us but that **it cannot dwell in an evil infested environment.** We must also learn what **God** considers sin and then look deeply into ourselves to uncover, acknowledge and overcome which sins live in **our** heart. After we acknowledge those sins, we must have remorse for them and seek forgiveness for them in order to be forgiven and begin to overcome them. This allows us to provide the Holy Spirit with a place within us where He can dwell. This means that we have to "get right" with God and will need to know what we must do to attain this goal.

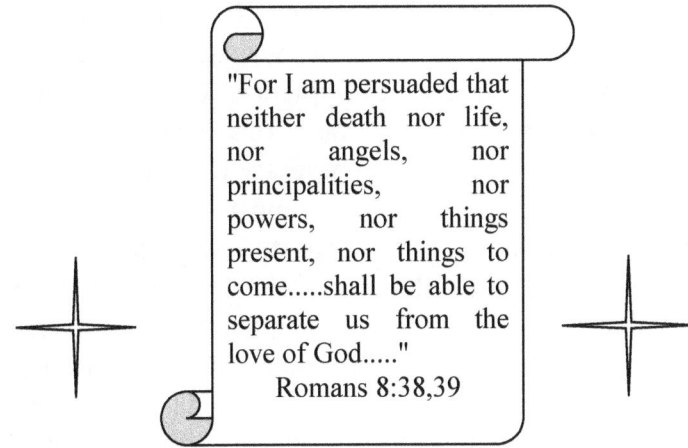

"For I am persuaded that neither death nor life, nor angels, nor principalities, nor powers, nor things present, nor things to come.....shall be able to separate us from the love of God....."
Romans 8:38,39

Chapter Nine

GETTING RIGHT WITH GOD

It is impossible to please God if we do not know what He asks of us, why we must adhere to His principles, and what He plans for our future. It is impossible for mankind to understand the enormity of what the future holds without knowing what God has done and will do. Sadly, so few understand that God has a created a plan for developing mankind into those who desire to be free of all things evil; those who will love Him and love who He loves. And what many cannot understand is that when God's Plan of Salvation is completed, a bride for His Son and inhabitants for His new kingdom will have been developed, and sadly, that **those who have rejected God's offer will not and _cannot_ be a part of this future** and face hell. The plan is specific and is, at this moment, open to everyone who was ever conceived, born or died. But we are fast approaching the time when grace will no longer be available.

God will create a new kingdom which He will fill with souls who understand the value of love, trust, honesty and loyalty, and will choose to practice these attributes voluntarily through their free will. This Plan of Salvation began when God created this temporary earth in its limited universe. God then created Adam and Eve to be the first souls who would be given the opportunity to develop into those who would seek the purity of love which allows the special relationships God desires to flourish. However, as mentioned in an earlier chapter, when God announced His plans for mankind, the beautiful and powerful angel Lucifer, later known as Satan, rebelled because he was deeply offended that God would provide mankind with a higher rank than the angels. Lucifer had already become jealous of Christ, and of the position Christ held by sitting at the right hand of God and now he became jealous of the new being which God wanted to bring to fruition. Satan's jealousy brought him to rebellion and he waged war against God and was eventually thrown to earth with the angels who joined his rebellion. Lucifer then became known as Satan.

Satan understands God's plan and knows that when God obtains the number of souls He wants for His new kingdom, he and his followers will be thrown into hell for the evil brought against God and mankind. To prevent God's plan from coming to fruition, Satan damaged God's relationship with Adam and Eve by enticing them to sin. His goal was to force God to banish them as He had banished Satan, hoping this would slow or thwart God's Plan of Salvation. But God, knowing what Satan would do, provided a way for mankind to return to God by teaching them the difference between good and evil. However, the righteousness under which God has chosen to fulfill His Plan of Salvation demanded that the captivity under which Satan placed sinners be paid by a ransom which would forgive those sins. Christ offered to pay that ransom by giving His perfect, sinless life for mankind's freedom. Satan accepted this challenge believing that when Christ walked this earth he could cause Christ to sin. But Christ, who would remain **without sin**, did give His life as the perfect sacrifice by which the sins of man could be forgiven. Satan then dedicated himself to interfering with God's plan, trying to break the faith of those who would follow God to delay his being bound forever. Thus **Satan is fighting for his continued freedom when discouraging the faithful**.

Wanting all men to be saved, God also provided for those who **died in sin** by creating a means of **testimony in eternity** while grace is still available on earth. When Christ triumphed over death on the cross, He entered Hades for three days to give testimony of His triumph to sinners who had died before Christ brought His perfect sacrifice. *("He descended into Hell and on the third day rose again.....")* While in Hades, Christ told these unredeemed souls that now they too could find forgiveness through grace if they had a truly repentant heart.

God has allotted a certain amount of time for His children to be made ready. Only He knows when that time frame will end. (Matthew 24:36; Acts 1:7) When that time is up, Christ will return to earth to take the faithful to heaven with Him. This event is called "The First Resurrection" and those from eternity who had obtained forgiveness and those alive who are faithful will take part in this event. (James 1:18; 1 John 5:4; Revelation 2:7, 11, 26; Revelation 3:5, 12, 21, Revelation 12:5 and 11; Revelation 21:7) When they are gone, grace will be removed from the earth and will no longer be available to those who remain, nor to those in Hades, and a great destruction will begin where one third of all the people on earth will die. (Daniel 12:1-2; Matthew 24:21-22; Thessalonians 2:1-4; 2 Timothy 3:1-9)

Three and one half years later, when the destruction ends, God will send His Son back to earth with those He had taken at the First Resurrection. They will all have celestial bodies and will reign as kings and priests for one thousand years of peace during which testimony will be given to everyone living or dead who were not taken in the First Resurrection. Satan will be bound during this time, unable to influence mankind, so all mankind will learn about... **and accept...** God's offer. (Revelation 20:2; Isaiah 4:2-6; Isaiah 11; Isaiah 12; Daniel 2:44; Daniel 7:27; Amos 9:11-15) Those who receive this testimony will not have the opportunity to become a part of the Bride of Christ because the Bride was formed from those who Christ had taken at the First Resurrection. But **these remaining souls *will* be given the opportunity to become an inhabitant of God's new kingdom**.

After the one thousand years of peace has been completed, Satan will be loosed so those who accepted God's offer during this time period can be tested. (Revelation 20:7-10) Satan, knowing that his time is almost up, will wreak havoc on those not firm in their faith and many will fall. Then, Judgment Day will come (John 5:22; Revelation 20:12-14) when everyone, *except* those taken by Christ for the First Resurrection, will be judged by what they did or did not do during their lifetime. Those taken by Christ at the First Resurrection will reign as kings and priests in the new kingdom and will not be judged because their sins had been forgiven. But those not taken at that time but who will receive testimony during the thousand years of peace **will** face judgment. Scripture tells us that this judgment will separate the "goats" from the "lambs". The "goats," will be cast into hell with Satan forever for what is called **the second death** which is **torment for all eternity**. Those who are deemed to be the "lambs" will go to heaven to live outside the City where the Royal Family of God will reside. **The goats, along with all evil and all hate will be bound forever with Satan and his demons, never to harm God's children again.** (Revelation 21:1-4)

To re-cap, it is important to remember that a **specific amount of time has been allotted in God's Plan of Salvation for His chosen ones to be made ready.** (Acts 1:6-7) When that time is up, God will send His Son to earth for those who will be a part of the First Resurrection (Revelation 20:5). When they are gone, grace will also be gone, and the final destruction of the end times will begin on earth and **one-third of all the people on earth will die.** When the destruction ends, God will send His Son back to earth with those He had taken at the First Resurrection. They will reign with Christ as kings and priests for one thousand years and bring testimony to everyone living or dead who was not taken in the First Resurrection.

Satan will be bound during this time, unable to influence mankind, so all will learn about and accept God. But, after the one thousand years of peace, Satan will be loosed again so those who received testimony and accepted God during the thousand years of peace can be tested. (Revelation 20:7) Satan will wreak havoc on those not firm in their faith and many will fall and follow Satan again. (Revelation 20:2) Then the Day of Judgment will arrive when everyone will be judged, *except* those taken by Christ in the First Resurrection. **Those who remain faithful after Satan is loosed again, scripture calls the "lambs", and they will be allowed to occupy the new heaven God is creating. But those who did not remain faithful and fell to Satan again when he was loosed, scripture calls the "goats", and they will be cast into hell with Satan and the fallen angels to be tormented day and night forever.** (Revelation 20:10 and 15)

Jude 1:6 tells us: *"And **the angels which kept not their first estate, but left their own habitation, he hath reserved in everlasting chains** under darkness unto the judgment of the great day,"*

Those who will enter God's new kingdom will either be a part of God's Royal Family and live inside the city gates or be those who live in other parts of Heaven as the lambs who accepted Christ during the thousand years of peace and remained faithful after Satan was loosed again. The Royal Family of God is referred to in scripture as the firstfruits, firstlings, overcomers, and as the Bride of Christ. These souls are also mentioned in the Apocrypha. 11 Esdras 2:40-41 says, *"Receive thy number O Sion, and embrace those of thine that are clothed in white which have fulfilled the law of the Lord. **The number of thy children whom thou longest for, is fulfilled:** beseech the Lord that thy people, which have been called from the beginning, may be hallowed."*

As we seek God and learn His words, we must remember that Satan loves the anonymity of working in secret. He wins when we succumb to hate, when we judge, condemn, gossip, are complacent, think that we know better than scripture, or bask in our own limited understanding. Satan is so subtle that many cannot believe that he exists, or that his fallen angels bring such harm. Genesis 3:1 tells us, *"….. the serpent was more **subtil** than any beast……"* Scripture teaches us that Satan is a liar, a murderer (of men's souls), and is subtle in his attacks, and that he walks this earth to influence mankind. Matthew 4:1 adds that Satan tempts us. *"Then was Jesus led…… to be tempted of the devil."* And in Matthew 4: 3 *"and when the tempter came to Him, he said….."* Thus we know that Satan has power, is unscrupulous, and wants to separate us from God; we know that the fallen angels who work with Satan also tempt and lie and are subtle in their attacks. All men sin, but if they are contrite and repent with true remorse, God will forgive them. God's plan is to fill His kingdom with souls who will truly love **one another**, and love His Son and Him **above all else.**

But to reach the goal of our faith which is to become a part of God's kingdom, scripture warns that we are not to trust our own understanding because it is so limited and so easily influenced by Satan. Scripture teaches us that we must **trust God's words** and follow His statutes to escape what Satan can do. Proverbs 3:5-7 says: "*Trust in the Lord with all your heart and* **lean not unto thine own understanding.** *In all ways acknowledge Him and He shall make thy paths.* **Be not wise in thine own eyes**...."

False doctrines will abound in the time just before Christ returns, and may also come "from within" or by "those among us". In fact, many of these doctrines are so benign that it is difficult not to succumb to them. Some teach that all we have to do is "believe". Some teach that "works" and how we conduct our lives on a day to day basis is not that important. Many do not teach that to have our sins forgiven carries certain pre-requisites nor do they teach that God warns us not to take Holy Communion unworthily. 1 Corinthians 11:27-29 warns: "*Wherefore whosoever shall eat this bread and drink this cup of the Lord,* **unworthily shall be guilty**.......*But* **let a man examine himself.....For he that eateth and drinketh unworthily, eateth and drinketh damnation to himself....**"

Sadly, we look at other churches, other doctrines, and other leaders without considering that **the powerful warning against false doctrines must also be applied to the circles in which we personally travel.** The strength of this admonition is evidenced by its similar words in other passages throughout the Holy Bible. Scripture tells us that God Himself inspired the words of the Bible by sending His Holy Spirit to work in the heart of those who wrote, translated and published this incredible Book. In creating the Bible, the Holy Spirit worked through two kings (David and Solomon), two priests (Jeremiah and Ezekiel), one physician (Luke), two fishermen (Peter and John), two shepherds (Moses and Amos), one Pharisee and theologian (Paul), one statesman (Daniel), one tax collector (Matthew), one soldier (Joshua), one scribe (Ezra), one butler (Nehemiah), and others. **All scripture** is the Divine Word of our living God, thus what we see and hear in this world must be compared to what scripture tells us. In fact, we are very clearly warned in Revelation 22:18-19: *"if any man shall take away from the words of the book of this prophecy,* **God shall take away his part out of the book of life,** *and out of the holy city, and from the things which are written in this book".* 2 Timothy 3:15-16 tells us: *"And that from a child thou hast known* **the holy scriptures, which are able to make thee wise unto salvation........**All scripture **is given by inspiration of God***, and is profitable for doctrine, for reproof, for correction,* **for instruction in righteousness**". Satan, in his effort to delay the completion of God's plan, works to separate man from God by condoning sin, ignoring sin in others, encouraging our arrogance in thinking that we are righteous, that scripture is not accurate, and that our works are not a marker of our relationship with God. Satan works to make us doubt that scripture is the word of God and produces the arrogance from which one finds fault with its words. But scripture teaches us to trust its words and believe that they are the word of God. Scripture teaches us that obtaining grace requires us to **acknowledge our sins and strive to overcome them.** We are to share what we learn about God's words with others....and *"lean not unto our own understanding".*

The Bible tells us that we must "teach, rebuke, and exhort" what we have learned of God's words **and exercise the four pre-requisites for obtaining the forgiveness of sin;** *acknowledge our sins, have remorse for having committed them, honestly desire to overcome them, and forgive others.* We must not fall prey to Satan's words which tell us **"surely God didn't mean."** 2 Corinthians 11:14 clearly warns: **"Believe not every spirit for Satan masquerades as an angel of light".** Many of those who think they know what God expects of them do not know.... and sadly, they will be like the five foolish virgins when Christ returns. They will be surprised that they are not taken. But like Adam and Eve, they meant well. They did not set out to destroy their relationship with God. They were drawn into disobeying God because of the subtle and well worded argument which Satan placed in their hearts or the conceit of leaning to their own understanding. The same ploy is used today by Satan and therefore God asks us to examine our deeds daily to see if there is love and compassion and support in every one of them. We also need to help one another grow in faith and in loving deeds for <u>**if we condone or encourage one another's sins, we are just as guilty of that sin as they are**</u>.

Scripture tells us in Matthew 24:42: *"Watch therefore;* ***for ye know not what hour your Lord doth come."*** God desires that *all* men be saved and **He brings testimony to <u>everyone</u> in one form or another.** But as we read scripture, and these parables and the words of the Apostles, we learn that though many are called, many either **will *not* accept** God's words nor His invitation, or **will not follow** God's statutes, and thus **will not be "made ready".** Matthew 24:36 tells us, *"But of that day and hour* **knoweth no man**...*but my Father only."* We also read that those who will be left behind will be in great agony. Matthew 22:13 says, *"…. **there shall** *be weeping and gnashing of teeth."* Scripture also tells us about the signs we will see as we approach the end times. Matthew 24:4-12,24 tell us, *"....wars, rumours of wars, famine, pestilences, earthquakes in diverse places, hatred toward Christians, betrayals, hatred, false prophets with signs and wonders, iniquity, no love"*

Luke 21: 25 explains, *"And there shall be signs in the sun, and in the moon, and in the stars....the sea and the waves roaring....Men's hearts failing them for fear...."* And 2 Timothy 3:1-7 tells us, *"...in the last days perilous times shall come. For men shall be lovers of their own selves, covetous, boasters, proud, blasphemers, disobedient to parents, unthankful, unholy. Without natural affection, trucebreakers, false accusers, incontinent, fierce, despisers of those that are good. Traitors, heady, high minded, lovers of pleasures more than lovers of God;* **Having a form of godliness but denying the power thereof....ever learning, and never able to come to the knowledge of the truth."**

2 Esdras 16:24 from the Apocrypha adds: *"At that time shall* **friends fight** *one against another..."* 1 Thessalonians 4:16 tells us, *"For the Lord himself shall descend from heaven with a shout....then we....shall be caught up....to meet the Lord in the air....."* 1 Thessalonians 5:2 warns: *"For yourselves know perfectly that the day of the Lord so cometh as a thief in the night."* 2 Peter 3:10, 14 tells us, *"But the day of the Lord will come as a thief in the night.....Wherefore, beloved, seeing that ye look for such things,* **be diligent that ye** *may* **be found** *of him in peace,* **without spot, and blameless."**

Revelation 9:6 tells us, **"And in those days shall men seek death and shall not find it, and shall desire to die, and** death shall flee from them." Matthew 24:21, 22 warns, *"For then shall be great tribulation, such as was not since the beginning of the world to this time, no, nor ever shall be. And except those days should be shortened, there should no flesh be saved: but for the elect's sake those days shall be shortened."*

But, we can be comforted by God's words in Revelation 2:10 where He tells us: *"**Fear none of those things which thou shalt suffer….**"* And in Luke 12:32: *"Fear not, little flock; For it is your Father's good pleasure to give you the kingdom."* If we are faithful and strive to learn of God and follow His precepts, we will experience the wonderful promise God reveals in Revelation 21:4: *"And God shall wipe away all tears from their eyes; and there shall be no more death, neither sorrow, nor crying, **neither shall there be any more pain…..**"* Matthew 25:21 comforts us with the words: *"…..**thou hast been faithful** over a few things, I will make thee ruler over many..."*

Getting right with God requires **knowing God's plan and believing it; trusting it.** It would be so nice if we could snap our fingers to obtain such knowledge and conviction. But the truth is, this takes work on our part and **it is a fight from the day we realize the battle in which we are engaged to the time when God calls us home.** Even the Apostles of old acknowledged that they would need to **run the race and fight the fight** right up to the end of their lives. 2 Timothy 4:7 tells us: *"I have fought the good fight, I have finished the race, **I have kept the faith.**"*

Hebrew 10:23-25 tells us: *"Let us **hold fast the profession of our faith without wavering**: (for he is faithful that promised:) And let us consider one another to provoke* *unto love and to good works. Not forsaking the assembling of ourselves together, as the manner of some is; but **exhorting one another:** and so much the more, as ye see the day approaching.* These words tell us to continue to learn God's words, share them with one another, and invite others to hear them. We are to support one another whenever we waver, and encourage one another to work toward the day of Christ's return. We must keep our faith alive and ask God to increase our faith. Revelation 14:15 reminds us of the moment God tells Christ to fetch His bride with the words: *"....Thrust in thy sickle and reap; for the time is come for thee to reap; for **the harvest of the earth is ripe**."*

Getting right with God begins with a desire to share in the future God offers. We must remember that to obtain this future will require that **our faith be tested. Therefore we will have to be firmly rooted in God's words to withstand that test.** Knowing God, believing what He says and seeking to obey His statutes will keep us strong. When we have passed that test and proven our faith, God's reward will be ours.

Romans 15:4 reminds us: *"For whatsoever things were written aforetime were written **for our learning**, that we **through patience** and comfort **of the scripture** might have hope.* Therefore, as we learn what God plans for those who choose to follow Him, we begin **to desire** to make changes in our lives and can more easily and quickly recognize our errors. When this happens, we begin **to work** on reducing those mistakes. We learn **to act** as soon as the wrong thought enters our mind. Through this process we also begin **to allay** and then finally **to prevent** the fear which Satan wants to plant in our mind....and we begin **to move** in the direction of being an overcomer.

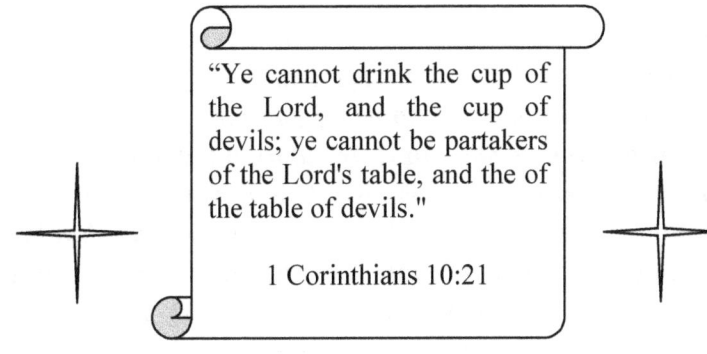

"Ye cannot drink the cup of the Lord, and the cup of devils; ye cannot be partakers of the Lord's table, and the of the table of devils."

1 Corinthians 10:21

Chapter Ten

THE OVERCOMER

There is not anything which occurs in our life that God is not aware of. While we do bring many situations upon ourselves, others are brought to us by Satan and even then, God is watching and wants to help. If we have opened our heart to God we know that He will embrace us with His incredibly loving and forgiving nature. His love for us is evident through the marvelous future He has worked so hard to provide for us. Nevertheless, sorrow, pain, heartache and loss are often the better teachers for mankind because pain makes us sit up and take notice of how we handle adversity and how sincerely we seek God. Sadly, it is our suffering which seems to be the most effective way for us to learn. It is often the best form of instruction; and in time teaches us that **God uses everything in our life for our edification.** If we trust this truth, we can endure our hardships under the hope that from our pain we will grow spiritually. We can believe more effectively that God is developing our souls to become the Bride of Christ or a lamb in His kingdom. Therefore, we can welcome our struggles as an opportunity to obtain the goal of an eternity with our Heavenly Father. We may also desire to learn quickly so the hardships we deal with over our current concerns can come to an end. Revelation 2:10 tells us: **"Fear none of those things which thou shalt suffer**: behold **the devil shall cast some of you into prison; that ye may be tried; and ye shall have tribulation** ten days: **be thou faithful unto death, and I will give thee a crown of life**." And Revelation 4:11 tells us: Behold, I come quickly; **hold that fast which thou hast; that no man take thy crown."** The words "hold fast" tell us that we must work to the very end to maintain our faith; to retain the crown of glory for which we have laboured. However, to achieve the goal of our faith we must work to become an overcomer and this can only be attained if we **willingly seek to learn what God wants to tell us**. Revelation 3:6, 13, and 22 repeat the words: "He that hath an ear, **let him hear** what the Spirit sayeth unto the churches......". By hearing what God's Plan of Salvation is all about, by asking God to open our understanding, and by availing ourselves of the sacraments God offers, we learn about God and the future He wants us to have. As we strive to overcome the temptation of sin, and free ourselves of the pain Satan wants to bring us, we must align ourselves with Christ.

Revelation 3:5 makes us the promise: **"He that overcometh**, the same shall be clothed in white raiment; and I will not blot out his name in the book of life, **but I will confess his name before my Father,** and before the angels." And Psalm 18: 17-19 adds: *"***He delivered me** *from my strong enemy, and from them which hated me; for* ***they were too strong for me.*** *They prevented me in the day of my calamity; but the Lord was my stay. He brought me forth also into a large place;* ***he delivered me, because he delighted in me."*** But **to be an overcomer means that we must not only fight against the fears and thus the reaction to fear which Satan places in our heart, but also love God and those He loves.**

SATAN'S GIFT OF FEAR

Matthew 22:37-39 tells us: *"Jesus said unto him, Thou shalt love the Lord thy God with **all thy heart, and with all thy soul, and with all thy mind.** This is the first and great commandment. And the second is like unto it, Thou shalt **love thy neighbor as thyself.**"* Sadly, life is now terribly demanding because of the great strides Satan has made in this world. He can blind us to our shortcomings and prevent us from recognizing that, rather than love others, we actually bring them harm. Gossip, unkind references, a refusal to help those we see who need help, a self-interest so strong that we cater only to our own needs, the envy we carry toward others, and even being a bad example to others is a sin in God's eyes. To be an overcomer means that we no longer succumb to *everything* Satan brings into our lives, especially fear and anxiety. It means that when God brought His admonitions to our attention we listened! As we learned His words and understood what He was asking of us, we desired to change. We began the work that was necessary on ourselves to **overcome our actions and reactions of the past**. In fact, we may have even tried to make restitution for any harm we might have caused in the past. These prove our trust in God as well. Those attributes, in God's eyes, make up the overcomer. Overcoming the fear Satan places in our hearts, overcoming envy, overcoming our inherited sins, overcoming those habits we so easily fall into which displeases God, trusting Him, all adds up to what God considers an overcomer. Sadly, without the tools to fight, and the desire to keep on trying even when we fail, we cannot achieve this goal.

When we fall in love, we want to please the one we love. We desire to learn what they like to do, where they like to go, what they like to eat, what they like to wear, what they enjoy talking about. We seek ways to let them know that we love them and we support them in their goals. Falling in love with God is no different. We need to learn what God wants, what His plan is for us, how we can please Him. We want to talk to God; really communicate with Him about our life together, about what we can do to please Him, what adjustments we still need to make, and thank Him for loving us, for forgiving us, for protecting us, and for the plan He's made for our future. We need to let Him know how thankful we are for His Plan of Salvation and ask Him to help us be worthy to participate in it. Scripture provides us with analogies which help us comprehend the immense beauty of the new creation which those who remain faithful will enjoy. While many may enter this new world, it will be the Bride of Christ, those taken at the First Resurrection, who will live and reign at God's side. They are referred to as the "firstfruits" and also as the "overcomers", and the "kings" and "priests" of God's new world. They are a group of people, not a single person and are those who developed a close and loving relationship with their Heavenly Father and with Christ, who is referred to as the Bridegroom of their soul. To be a part of the Bride of Christ means that these souls will become the "daughter-in-law" to God and, as the culture of the days of Christ teaches, they will live in the same home which God and Christ will occupy. Thus these words and descriptions of those Christ will take at the First Resurrection and what they will be given teach us how closely tied to God and Christ these souls will be for all of eternity. **These souls are, in essence promised a place in God's home....inside the gates of the City of God which will contain God's "Royal Family".** The Bride of Christ are those who loved God and **demonstrated their love by striving to learn of Him, trust Him, and obey Him.** While on earth, they worked on themselves, and they worked in God's vineyard to help spread the Gospel.... and are being rewarded for that labour. 1 Corinthians 15:58 tells us, *"Therefore, my beloved brethren,* *be ye steadfast, <u>unmoveable</u>, always abounding in the work of the Lord, forasmuch as ye know that your labour is not in vain of the Lord."* Psalm 1:1-3 tells us, **"Blessed is the man** *that walketh not in the counsel of the ungodly, nor standeth in the way of sinners, nor sitteth in the seat of the scornful. But **his delight is in the law of the Lord;** and in his law doth he meditate **day and night**. And he shall be like a tree planted by the rivers of water, that bringeth forth his fruit in his season; his leaf also shall not wither, and whatsoever he doeth shall prosper."* Through these verses and many others, we learn who God will bless and what our behavior must be to be found worthy at the First Resurrection. Psalms 1:1 tells us: *"walketh not in the counsel of the ungodly......but **delight in the law of the Lord."*** God's children strive to overcome the self-serving Adam-like nature and develop a Christ-like nature to achieve this goal. They understand that a loving father who seeks a bride for his son would want that bride to be kind, longsuffering, loyal and forgiving. They know that scripture warns that **only** *half* **of those who <u>are believers</u> will meet the criteria required to become the Bride.** They know that not all believers will be taken at the First Resurrection thus will not become a part of the Bride of Christ; a part of the overcomers which the Bible speaks of. We need to clearly understand this truth so we will strive to shed our old nature, become more like Christ, desire to leave all things evil, learn to love, to trust God, teach these truths to our children and try to love others more completely. God sees **everything including the hidden recesses of our heart. He knows our motives and our faults and failings and He knows where we have given all we can.** God also knows our striving and hears our prayers to love more, to grow in compassion, to learn *and do* what He asks. The Bride of Christ will be expected to *desire* to be **perfect in her love toward others** by being, applying, developing, teaching, and giving love. God is touched by those who ask Him to help them be an overcomer and to grow into what will please Him.

When we love God, we want to spurn what is not righteous in the eyes of God. We long to serve God and be with Him for all eternity where love will reign and evil will not exist. **God wants us to be free of evil and to live with Him for all eternity in righteousness and love. He gives us every tool to do so and protects the path we must take to reach that goal. God's love for us is so great that He allowed His Son to sacrifice His life so we could be saved from the captivity of the sin which Satan brings us.** While sin dooms us to the Lake of Fire, God has given us the gift of scripture to help us learn how to avoid the life Satan offers. God wants *all* men to be saved and He wants us to succeed. He tells us in Jeremiah 31:3: *The Lord hath appeared of old unto me, saying Yea,* **I have loved thee with an everlasting love:** *therefore* **with loving kindness have I drawn thee.** And He tells us in Revelation 22:17: *"And the Spirit, and the bride say,* **Come** *and let him that* **heareth** *say, Come, and let him that is athirst come. And* **whosoever will, let him take the water of life freely.**" The words in Romans 16:20 bring us comfort through the promise: *"And* **the God of peace shall bruise Satan under your feet** *shortly."* Therefore, we should say as Joshua 24:15 says: *"...As for me and my house, we will serve the Lord"*. And while we wait we must... as John 16:33 and Acts 27:25 tell us: *"Be of good cheer"*. Being an overcomer is not something which we can see happening at first but then, when we are faced with sin, we suddenly realize that we have engaged our faith to spurn it. We see that our brains no longer respond to Satan's whispers and we no longer react to fear without thinking about God's protection, and.... we **no longer feel the anxiety we once felt over similar situations.** We trust that God will take care of us; trust that **He will bring a blessing out of every situation.**

The more we do overcome, the easier it gets. Immediately recognizing the sin which Satan lays before us is offering God something very special. God sees what we have achieved and will reward those efforts. We touch God's heart even more when we walk away from sins which might appear gratifying. And even if we entertain sinful thoughts for a short time but then do walk away from them, God remains faithful to us telling us in 1 John 1:9: *"If we confess our sins,* **he is faithful** *and just* **to forgive** *our sins and* **to cleanse** *us from all unrighteousness."* The true overcomer **desires** to do God's will and to love others and help where we can. James 2: 14 tells us: ***What doth it profit, my brethren, though a man say he hath faith, and have not works? Can faith save him? And in verse 17-18: Even so faith, if it hath not works, is dead, being alone.......I will show thee my faith by my works."*** Expressions of love are some of the "works" which God asks us to do. God has given us free will and has painstakingly provided every means by which we can learn of His offer. But **it will be entirely up to us to accept what He tells us and act on those words.....or not!** Our loving Heavenly Father **will forgive every sin for which we have remorse. God will help us be an overcomer. No effort will go unnoticed by God.** He loves us unconditionally and suffers when we suffer. But to bring us the future He has outlined, **He has chosen to work under the rules of righteousness** thus, when mankind fell to sin he became **destined to remain enslaved by sin unless he turns to God.** Scripture tells us that **all** men are sinners. Therefore, every one of us is a sinner and everyone has inherited the tendency to sin, **some of which we do not even recognize** until we search God's words and understand His nature. Pride, arrogance, complacency, conceit, <u>*self-justification*</u> and self-aggrandizement are just a few. Our lack of understanding causes our Heavenly Father great consternation and is why

He leaves no stone unturned to bring us His message and encourage us to learn of Him and trust His ways. ***All God asks of us is that we hear Him out; that we listen to His message*** and place it in our hearts. He will work with the little we can do on our own and will **help us recognize the truth and teach us how to find freedom from sin. But then....**we must do our part. Overcoming means that we build a closer relationship with God; that we talk to Him, learn of Him, tell Him our concerns, our hopes and dreams and wishes; thank Him for what He has done for us and what He offers us. Overcoming is recalling and thanking God for the blessings we have received and the joy we feel that we can talk with Him, continue to learn, and hope for the incredible future He offers us. Learning God's Plan of Salvation, learning what God considers sin, learning what the sacraments are, and why we need them, entering into prayer and conversation with God, and choosing to follow God's path of righteousness develops our faith, **removes our fear and anxieties** and helps us be an overcomer. Overcoming is also listing every past blessing and verbally thanking God for bringing us through everything we faced in the past. By doing this aloud, we condition our soul to withstand the fear that attacks us when we face a difficult circumstance. In time, that spirit of fear will leave and be replaced with the confidence that God will help us.

We will fail from time to time, but desiring and working toward overcoming our Adam-like nature and learning to recognize and avoid the traps which Satan lays for us truly does touch God's heart. Growing into that which God sees in us will bring us benefits which we cannot even imagine. We will no longer fear, no longer experience anxiety and have a single minded goal which will be realized sooner that we think. We will live in a wonderful new world free of evil, and full of joy!

Bibliography

The Holy Bible, King James Version, published by The New Apostolic Church, Canada, Thomas Nelson, Inc., Camden, NJ, 1972

James Strong, LLD, STD, *Strong's Exhaustive Concordance of the Bible*, Abington, Nashville, thirty fourth printing 1996, copyright 1890

Ray C. Stedman, *Spiritual Warfare*, Word Books, Publisher, Waco, Texas, 1976

Sophy Burnham, *A Book of Angels*, Ballantine Books, New York 1990

Henry H. Halley, *Halley's Bible Handbook,* Zondervan Publishing House, Grand Rapids, Michigan, 24th edition, Copyright 1965

Henry M. Morris, *Many Infallible Proofs*, Moody Press, Chicago, 3rd printing 1977

Henry M. Morris, *The Bible and Modern Science*, Moody Press, Chicago, 1951, 1968

Donald Grey Barnhouse, *The Invisible War,* Zondervan Publishing House, Grand Rapids, Michigan, 12th printing 1976 copyright 1965

Robert Boyd, *Boyd's Bible Handbook*, Eugene, Oregon: Harvest House, 1983

"....He shall

pluck

my feet

out

of the net."

Psalm 25:15

About The Author

Helen Glowacki is an interior designer, writer, teacher, and motivational speaker. She was the host, writer, and producer of the television series *"The Contemporary Woman"*, broadcast by UA Columbia Cablevision. Her writing credentials include an extensive background as a freelance feature and staff writer for four newspapers and for various newsletters, and a Christian Online Magazine. Helen was a guest on a conservative radio show and guest co-hosted a cable television game show. A graduate of William Paterson University, Helen received a Bachelor of Arts degree, magna cum laude, in Communications. She also received an Associate of Science degree with honors through which she became a registered nurse and she completed an apprenticeship as an Interior Designer.

Helen donates many of her books to cancer centers, drug rehabilitation centers, prisons, youth centers, and hospitals. She sends them to the mission schools of *The Henwood Foundation* of The New Apostolic Church in Lusaka, Zambia and to Sunday schools in Lahore, Pakistan. She emails books to those willing to receive testimony or will help in her quest to bring testimony to others. Helen writes inspiring and educational articles based in scripture which are filled with insight about how God wants us to conduct our lives. She posts many of these articles on Face Book and also on her website so others can use them in their personal testimony and teaching. Her speaking engagements have included nine cruise ships, adult living complexes, congregations in Lahore, Pakistan, High Schools and College Campuses. Her desire is to use her gift for writing to help others find the love and comforting presence of God.

Those who have provided reviews of Helen's books tout the beauty of the stories in her novels and often say that if you read one, you will want to read them all. While her novels progress as a saga, each is complete in itself and offers her readers a wonderful story of how one person can affect future generations.

Helen's non-fiction books have been said to be "spiritually uplifting, biblically correct and very educational". They address how scripture can be used in our everyday lives and how Satan works to thwart God's Plan of Salvation.

Helen's *"Why God Why"* mini-series of books are a quick and easy read on specific categories of scripture and an excellent educational and eye-opening tool for all ages. They are an excellent resource for testimony and fund raisers.

Helen's greatest joys have been her husband, her two children, four grandchildren, and time spent in her New Apostolic faith and in fellowship. Her hobbies are ballroom dancing, tennis, and interior design.

To order additional books, visit the author's website www.helenglowacki.com or Amazon.com. To become a distributor of these books, or to purchase in quantity for fund raisers or testimony, email the author at: helen@helenglowacki.com.

You can also visit her Face Book page at: http://www.facebook.com/pages/Helenglowacki/

Or view her book listings on Face Book at: http://www.facebook.com/pages/The-Grandmother-Series/155300907853909?ref=ts

Excerpt from Book 7 of the Why God Why Series:

What Do Angels Do?

As we study scripture we learn of the warning found in Revelation 1:19 which tells us: *"And if any man shall take away from the words of the book of this prophecy, God shall take away his part out of the book of life, and out of the holy city......".* This teaches us that we must use the words of scripture as authentically as we can, and always regard them as truth. We must check and double check the doctrines under which we sit by comparing them to what scripture tells us. We must work to apply even those things which may be the *perspectives* of the prophets as they relate the visions God provided to them. God also tells us that He will open the mysteries of scripture to those who seek the truth.

While it is not necessary to our soul salvation to learn about the heavenly hierarchy or the function of angels, it does provide us with a greater understanding of the incredible power which makes up our universe and which ultimately affects everything in our lives. While many disregard scripture, and others believe its words to be only mystical allegories impossible to apply, there are many who *do* believe scripture and use its directives to guide their lives.

Those who do trust scripture believe, as I do, that scripture is the word of God given to develop the Bride of Christ and that God will unveil even its most cryptic messages to those who truly desire to learn. In the book titled *"Why Trust Scripture"* in my Why God Why series of books I presented a variety of information which demonstrated how the words of scripture support both the Creation *and* the elements of carbon dating. Interestingly, that information highlighted the fallibility of man's interpretation of scripture and negated any scriptural inconsistency.

Another verse which may in time demonstrate the accuracy of scripture and our fallibility in terms of interpretation comes from a vision which the Apostle John was given about the end times. In Revelation 9:3,7,9 and 10 John wrote: *"And there came out of the smoke locusts upon the earth....and the shapes of the locusts were like unto horses prepared unto battle; and on their heads were as it were crowns like gold, and their faces were as the faces of men…..breastplates of iron, and the sound of their wings was as the sound of chariots of many horses....and they had tails like unto scorpions…..and their power was to hurt men five months."*

Some Biblical scholars believe that what John saw in this vision was a fleet of our modern day attack helicopters, while others believe that he saw the demons loosed from the abyss which Revelation 9:11 tells us Isaiah saw in his vision. The Apostle John, never having seen modern technology or this type of demonic activity, could only describe what he saw within the parameters of his limited experience. Nevertheless, those words stand today and are expected to become yet another testament to the perfect accuracy of scripture. Similarly when we read in Revelation 21:21: *"And the twelve gates were twelve pearls....and the street of the city was pure gold...."* we can accept that these words are an attempt to describe the incredible beauty of the city in heaven which will be created for the Bride of Christ. Whether the word "pearl" actually refers to the pearls we find inside a clam or whether it refers to a yet unknown substance which is as white and transparent and shiny as the pearls with which we are familiar doesn't really matter. Whether the word gold refers to streets paved with the gold the prophets recognized or with something which is as beautiful and valuable as the gold they referenced also does not matter.

What *does* matter is that we take from scripture those things which teach us about our future and how we can attain the understanding to prepare for that future through the perfection of our soul. Thus, whether allegory or fact, or whether couched in a mystery which is unveiled as we gain a better understanding of God's Plan of Salvation, we can believe that scripture constantly proves itself accurate. Therefore, as we read about angels and seek to understand their role in heaven and how they might impact *our* world, we must look into the words employed by those prophets who described their visions of angels with words found only through their limited perspective.

As we study this scripture, we learn that the *fallen* angels retained the powers they received in heaven and now use those powers *against* mankind. We learn about the theocracy under which we will live and why God requires that everything in the new heaven and earth be free of all things evil. We learn how everything we experience helps us through the spiritual growth process we undergo here on earth. We learn to appreciate the plan God has put into place to bring us a new world, free of evil, and filled with a populace who long to live in such an environment. We learn to embrace the breadth of diversity which God has wrought in those things He placed on earth, in heaven, and throughout His universe. We begin to recognize the immensity of God's plan for our future and the love with which He draws us. This helps us grow into a more selfless person with a desire to promote and share that love and an understanding about why we should put on the armour of protection God provides, watch for the influence of the fallen angels, and prepare ourselves for the First Resurrection.

Therefore, what we can learn about angels and the powers they exert over us, both for good and for bad, will help us spurn the evil Satan brings. Satan's goal is to separate us from God to extend his freedom and retain his power. Each of us must make that ever important decision to follow God, avoid Satan's trap of sin and complacency and work to shed the selfish Adam-like nature created when Satan caused Adam and Eve to sin... and which we inherited at birth. We must grow into the self-sacrificing Christ-like nature God will look for in the Bride. Therefore, we must learn to recognize the harm the fallen angels seek to do under Satan's directives. We can only accomplish this by learning *what* they do and *how* they do it.

Scripture teaches us that when the angels were created, God endowed them with certain powers and placed them into a hierarchy consisting of three major ranks. Each rank was empowered to perform a specific range of duties. The angels who remained faithful to God use these powers for the good of mankind while the fallen angels use them to harm man and impede his spiritual progress. Few people understand that the fallen angels who followed Satan in his rebellion against God *retained* their powers when they were banished from heaven. Therefore, whether Satan sends a fallen angel to harm us, or God sends a faithful angel to help us, each employ their powers when they interact with or for us.

Most angelic interventions are so subtle that we may not recognize their work. Therefore we often do not concern ourselves with the fact that Satan himself, who is the leader of the fallen angels, directs his followers to separate us from God. Satan's desire is to block our awareness that evil is real and active in our lives, and to place indifference in our hearts to prevent us from learning about God's plan of salvation. The angels who remain faithful to God help mankind battle these satanic spirits and use their powers to help us learn of God's offer, obtain the forgiveness of sin, and desire, as children of God, to develop into a worthy bride for His Son.

Certain ranks of angels can bring us the gifts of tenderness and hope, of healing and transformation, of various talents and service while the fallen angels pervert these attributes into cruelty and despair, sickness and false doctrines, complacency, fear and selfishness. Thus, as scripture teaches us about angels and the work they do; it also explains their duties and their powers while describing three spheres of heaven each of which contains three types of angels. The first sphere contains the *Seraphim*, the *Cherubim*, and the *Thrones* who have been given the power to **Counsel**. The second sphere contains the *Dominions*, the *Virtues,* and the *Powers* who have been given the power to **Govern**, and the third sphere contains the *Principalities*, the *Archangels*, and the *Angels* who act as **Messengers**.

"For the promise

is unto you,

and

to your children,

and to all

that are afar off,

even as many

as the Lord

our God shall call."

Acts 2: 39

Novels

<u>by Helen Glowacki</u>   (Book Size 6 x 9)

When God Broke Grandma's Heart: (208 pages) Rising from sorrow to become a beacon of faith Grandma struggles in an abusive marriage until God moves her from unequally yoked and broken to the healing of His love and forgiveness. Her granddaughter Sarah learns where to find answers to her problems and carries that legacy to those she loves. **Paperback: ISBN 978-0-9847-2110-8**

When God Took Grandma Home: (260 pages) About the heartache of drug addiction, of the enemy who destroys children through drugs, why God allows righteous anger, why we should pray for those in eternity and a description an incredible experience of faith for Matt and Sarah about why God allowed such heartache to occur. **Paperback: ISBN 978-0-49847-2111-5**

When Grandma Chased the Spirits: (208 Pages) The magnetism of idolatry, it's invisible power, and the heartache of bearing a child out of wedlock brings debilitating panic attacks to Mary and affects her husband Kevin. When Matt and Sarah tell them about their faith, God engineers a miracle to solve what that they thought impossible to resolve. **Paperback: ISBN 978-0-9847-2112-2**

The Granddaughter and the Monkey Swing: (284 pages) A wedding, a broken engagement, renovating and decorating a home through Divine Proportion, the truth about Halloween, and the gift of role models create a tender story of friendship. Helping through the planning and problems of a wedding culminates in the unveiling of a secret. **Paperback: ISBN 978-0- 9847-2113-9**

Grandma's Little Book of Poetry: The Story of God's Plan of Salvation: (277 pages) This original version which includes the poems is a beautiful whimsical story for all ages. It begins when Sarah finds a manuscript in Grandma's desk and recognizes the story Grandma read to her and Josh and Caleb when they were children. It is a story of how the inhabitants on the planet below the angels struggle to find God. **Paperback: ISBN 978-0-9847-2114-6**

Abiding Faith, Hidden Treasure: (262 pages) Serving in Iraq, Jim loses his faith to see a loving God allow so much heartache. Barbara invites him to dinner where Grandma shows him why creation and evolution co-exist and God's enemy creates the injustices Jim blames on God. Letters from the grave bring an incredible experience of faith. **Paperback: ISBN 978-0-9847-2115-3**

And Then They Asked God: (295 Pages) When Rebecca and Jayden arrive at their college campus they are overwhelmed by betrayal. Losing the values Rebecca once cherished fills her with guilt so monumental that she cannot forgive herself. Chaldeth the evil angel is defeated when God's grace frees Jayden and brings Rebecca's recovery. **Paperback: ISBN 978-0-9847-2116-7**

Caleb's Testimony: (262 pages) Caleb would have taken bets on his ability to trust God explicitly....until his accident. Now, he and Ann must face the wrath of Satan who wants them to blame God for their misfortune. Can they give up everything they worked for if God asks this of them? **Paperback: ISBN 978-0-9847-2119-1**

Coming Soon: *As Evil Prevails*

The "Why God Why" Series
by Helen Glowacki   (Book size: 5 ½ x 8 ½)

To What Purpose?: (126 pages) This first book in the *Why God Why* series answers questions about why we are here, what we need to learn, and what God plans for us. It is an excellent book for testimony and one you will share with others. **Paperback: ISBN 978-1-4507-7580-9**

Why God, Why?: (126 pages) This second book in the *Why God Why* Series describes why we experience heartache, its purpose, and how to face it. It answers questions about God's plan for us and what we need to do to be found worthy.
Paperback: ISBN 978-1-4507-7581-6

Why Trust Scripture?: (126 pages) This third book in the *Why God, Why* Series addresses the challenges against scripture, who wrote the Bible, the importance of the sacraments, what role Satan plays, and how health and the Bible are related.
Paperback: ISBN 978-1-4507-7582-3

What Should I Know about Life after Death and the Coming Tribulation?: (126 pages) What occurs following death, what will happen during the tribulation, and what the seven seals could mean to us are explained in this fourth book of the series. **Paperback: ISBN 978-1-4507-7583-0**

What Does God Want Me to do Right Now?: (126 pages) A concise explanation of what God asks of us, how we can live up to His expectations what is required to become a part of the Bride of Christ, and what God plans for the future with or without us. **Paperback: ISBN 978-1 4507-9076-5**

Do My Little Sins Really Count? (126 pages) Most of us believe that the little sins don't really matter but scripture explains why they do and teaches is about the seven deadly sins, sin by proxy, and sin by commission and omission which can affect whether or not we take Holy Communion worthily. **Paperback: ISBN: 978-0-9847-2117-7**

What Do Angels Do? (126 pages) Few of us know that there are three levels of heaven in which nine different ranks of angels exist. Nor do they know that these angels have been assigned three very different tasks. This little book takes the mystery out of what angel's do, who rules them, and how they affect our lives. **Paperback: ISBN: 978-0-9847-2118-4**

What is Faith? (126 pages) Faith increases as we increase our understanding of God's Plan for mankind. It is only through learning God's words that we can know what God asks of us and why. It is only through realizing that God is bound by His own rules of righteousness that we can find the key to increasing our faith and helping us become all that God wants us to become. **Paperback: ISBN: 978-0-9893-8076-8**

Satan's Gift of Fear: (126 pages) Fear affects millions of people and can cause anxiety of such magnitude that many must be medicated and are even debilitated by its affect. Interesting scripture is filled with over 350 verses which address this fear and many which tells us very explicitly why they exist. **Paperback: ISBN: 978-0-9893-8078-2**

Non-Fiction Books

By Helen Glowacki   (Book Size 5 ½ x 8 ½)

Politically Incorrect: The Get Some Gumption Handbook For When Enough is Enough: (406 pages) Fifty timely and controversial issues are examined under the politically correct approach and compared to what scripture tells us is the approach that God wants His children to take. **Paperback: ISBN 978-1-4507-9074-1**

Overcoming Depression: How To Be Happy: (258 pages) We all face heartache, and all feel sad from time to time. But depression lingers and can result from many different causes. It can rob us of hope and destroy our relationship with God. Thus our Heavenly Father tells us through scripture how we can tap into His blessing and His direction and brings joy out of tribulation. **Paperback: ISBN 978-1-4507-9077-2**

What No One Tells You About Addictions: (216 pages) From generational sin to the spiritual warfare in which we are engaged, and from why Satan uses addiction to the merits of tough love, this book is a must read. Why we do not understand the selfish co-dependency of the enabler, and what scripture tells us about spiritual invasion makes this one you will want to share. **Paperback: ISBN 978-1- 4507-9075-8**

"As For Me

and

My House,

We will

Serve

The Lord"

Joshua 24:15

Book Reviews

Reverend (District Apostle Ret.) Richard C. Freund, President of The New Apostolic Church, USA, Sea Cliff, New York: Magnificent writer, a story which makes the reader become emotionally involved, a joy to read, strong Christian values. *"When God Broke Grandma's Heart"*, best seller quality.

Reverend (District Apostle Ret.) Richard C. Freund, President of The New Apostolic Church, USA. Helen's new novel, *"When God Took Grandma Home"* "Delights, brings comfort to those who grieve. Inspires, gives insight into the after-life, masterful portrayal.

Reverend Andrew Muliokela: New Apostolic Church in Alexandria, Virginia, formerly from Zambia Africa: *The Granddaughter and the Monkey Swing* and this series of books are awesome! A journey unlike another, I was reading a great novel, learning about confidence, love and support but also learning Bible verses at the same time! Helen Glowacki teaches through her books and I recommend them 100%. You'll enjoy the journey!

Reverend Frederick Rothe, (Ret. New Apostolic Church, New York) Palm Beach Gardens Congregation, Florida: Spent 48 years serving God and another 30 in the congregation. These books contain an accurate account of what God wants of us and why we suffer. The application of scripture and the people in the stories stand for the principles God wants in all of us.

Reverend Kevin Speranza, New Apostolic Church, Palm Beach Gardens, Florida: *And Then They Asked God.* So happy I read this, weaves, documents biblical precepts, addresses political correctness, moral & political corruption, biased teaching, insidious growth of socialism renamed progressivism, self-importance, guilt and its debilitating power. WELL DONE! Identifies danger, artfully and Biblically addresses them.

Reverend Luke Jansen, Sr. V. P., Medical Connections, Boca Raton, Florida: "To Ms. Glowacki, author of **The Grandma Series**: grateful for your books, refreshing to find a Christian author who sees the *difference* between religion and spirituality AND that the two can and should be used in the same sentence.

Reverend Derryck Beukes, Montana-De Aar Congregation, Northern Cape, South Africa: Dear Helen, I personally often use your articles in my soul care visits, especially where youth are involved. I can assure you that your articles made a difference to my way of thinking, and I am busy encouraging fellow priests to read your works, as they are so factual and insightful! Thank you for your hard work. I thank God for you, and the wisdom He gave you! Please continue with the excellent work.

Deacon Shadreck Wilima, Overspill Congregation, Ndola, Zambia: Your articles prompt realistic examples which New Apostolic Christians need for their everyday living.

Youth Chairperson, Sunday School Teacher, Mulenga Ernest, Lusaka Central Congregation, Lusaka, Zambia: Through your writing I am constantly reminded of what to be aware of. I pray that God keeps you in the hollow of His hand, guards you and guides you to reach your brethren as you do me. Thanks for caring for the souls of many.

Reverend Aurelio Cerullo, Atripalda Congregation in Campania, Southern Italy: Dear Helen, your books and articles, and social networking bring brothers and sisters the words of our faith and touch the hearts of those who do not know our faith. Our goal is found through the grace of the apostolate and in this sense, the word's from 1 Corinthians 15:58 assumes an important meaning: *"Therefore, my beloved brethren, be steadfast, immovable, always abounding in the work of the Lord, Knowing That your labor is not in vain in the Lord".* Now that I am a minister of God for about a year I too am grateful to our beloved Father in Heaven for having opened the eyes of my soul, for having removed the plugs from my ears of my heart to hear and listen to His will in connection and communion with those who precede us, guided by the light of the Holy Spirit. God's work always evolves and adapts to the times and even via computers, cell phones and smart phones. I Thank God for having been able to know you, you're a very valuable pearl. God bless you richly.

Rev. Fred Krueger, (Ret.) Lutheran Minister 12 yrs and Clinical Social Worker 26 years, Dallas, Texas: "Inspiring, grabs the heart, author headed to the bestseller list, a pleasure to read, masterful. *"When God Took Grandma Home"* filled with insight into God's plan!

NOTE: The articles which are referred to in these reviews are excerpts from Helen Glowacki's non-fiction books. Not shown are reviews by the ministers who oversee *The Henwood Foundation*'s New Apostolic Mission Schools in Zambia and the ministers in Pakistan who review all reading materials prior to distribution.

Edith Stier, wife of a Ret. District Evangelist, Clifton, New Jersey: *The Grandma Series* helps those in need, inspirational, heartwarming, ends with a beautiful example of how God explains our pain, renews hope, shows us the way, creates miracles. I love this series.

Patricia Robinson, wife of a Ret. Rector, Indiana: 5 star rating: *When God Broke Grandma's Heart*: WONDERFUL INSPIRATIONAL NOVEL, enjoyed this book, well written, Bible references, how to achieve peace of mind and soul.

Rosemarie Schaal, wife of an Ret. Reverend, New York: *Abiding Faith, Hidden Treasure*: Reader develops empathy, feels emotion, hears a battle between scientific and spiritual knowledge. Skillful, detailed, brilliant, vivid, teaches that nothing happens that is not planned by Him.

Colette van Loggerenberg, wife of a Minister, Scottsville Congregation of Pietermaritzberg, South Africa: *Grandma's Little Book of Poetry: The Story of God's Plan of Salvation:* This has to be one of the BEST EVER books that I have read....If you ever get the chance to get one of Helen's novels...READ IT. It's like a fairytale but a TRUE fairytale.....Close your eyes and picture this: Grandma with her hair in a bun, glasses perched delicately on her nose, sitting in a rocking chair and her grandchildren sitting on the floor with BIG eyes hanging onto her every word.....but with a twist!!!!! If you have doubts about PRAYER...read this book. I LOVED IT...thank you!

Debbie Espeland, wife of a Rector, Palm Beach Gardens Congregation, Florida: 5 star rating: *When God Took Grandma Home:* HEARTWARMING! This book touched my heart. It is both heartwarming and very spiritual.

Aletta Venter, wife of a Deacon, Scottsville Congregation, Pietermaritzburg, South Africa: *"Grandma's Little Book of Poetry: The Story of God's Plan of Salvation".* What a learning process for me. Oooh I just **love** the way the angels are telling the story, **very original!** When is mankind ever going to learn? The inhabitant's lesson was to learn of good and evil. And they failed miserably each time. The devil has his agenda, and the inhabitants are the target. They call upon God for help, the angels rejoiced. Great....!!!

Aletta Venter, wife of a Deacon, Pietermaritzburg, South Africa: *"Abiding Faith, Hidden Treasure"* is the deepest and most rewarding novel I have ever read, touched my soul, made me cry, author's understanding of God's work is astounding, opens the mysteries

Lisa Mayo, wife of Minister, Palm Beach Gardens Congregation, Florida: Helen's *Why God Why* series of books gave me a new understanding of my faith. They are informative, so enlightening and in-depth, but in a way that is easily understood!!

Tammera Shelton, M.S. Psychology, Odenton, Maryland: I find *"When God Broke Grandma's Heart"* inspirational, beautifully portrays need to let go of negative events and that despite injustice, no pain is for naught.

Robert W. Rothe, USMC 1970-1976, Nevada: 5 star rating: *When God Broke Grandma's Heart:* Outstanding writer, kept me riveted, an angel sent to help through trying days. Thank you for helping me find peace.

Katharina Leipp, Schopfheim, Germany: This is the first time I have ever heard of a female New Apostolic author and I am very impressed by your articles. I have sent your link to my Shepherd and German friends and would like you to consider advertising in our German *Our Family Magazine.*

Claudine Visagie, South Africa: I'm trying to think of a way to introduce Helen's books and articles to others... especially to our youth. They are life changing!

Rabecca Mukuta Mukato, Lusaka, Zambia, Africa: Speaking on behalf of my Dad, District Elder Mukato, your articles are brilliant because they have changed me! Because of your articles my Dad has less headaches!

Robert Henry Parkes, Pietermaritzburg, South Africa: You are gifted with the verses and writings you do and are so inspiring to others. God is really using you as His special servant. You are really a wonderful person and we thank the Lord for you our sister in faith.

Frank Geores, from Port St. Lucie, Florida: *"When Grandma Chased The Spirits:* beautiful spiritual experience, can see caring nature and loving heart of author, eloquently reveals her love for God and search for truth. Worthy of the Star of Bethlehem rating. Thank you for sharing your magnificent gift.

Ben Lodwick, Avid Reader., from Brookfield, Wisconsin: Wow! An eye opener about God's plan of salvation, and why bad things happen to good people. Reminds me of Jim LaHaye and Jerry B. Jenkins "Left Behind Series". MUST READ!"

Dr. Walter Forman From North Palm Beach, Florida: *Grandma's Little Book of Poetry: The Story of God's Plan of*

Salvation: a "wonderful book about success and failure in life. All Helen's novels are wonderful, a balm for the soul and an education to the seeker."

Susan Day, From Jupiter, Florida: ***Abiding Faith, Hidden Treasure*** : I hated to put it down, couldn't wait to pick it up, read all Helen's books, proves every point, shows what to do through God's words. I am 90 and Helen's books have helped me call on God.

Georgette Rothe, From Fort Piece, Florida: ***Abiding Faith, Hidden Treasure*** was more than I expected; a Biblical course making you re-evaluate your beliefs, enjoyed the journey very much.

Fred D'Alauro, from Palm Beach Shores, Florida: Internet 5 star rating: ***When God TookGrandma Home:*** Remarkable! Inspirational, moving. Fascinating storyteller with a real message.
Debra Forman, Chester, New York. Internet 5 star rating: ***When God Broke Grandma's Heart****:* Written from the heart, shares the strong beliefs that shelters us in times of need, courage captivates the reader. Thank you.

Anonymous: Internet 5 star rating: ***When God Broke Grandma's Heart****:* WHEN LIFE GETS YOU DOWN, PICK THIS BOOK UP, it wrapped its arms around me. A wonderful read. Congratulations on an inspiring work.

A reviewer, a reader in Kentucky: Internet 5 star rating: ***When God Broke Grandma's Heart****:* Well written, heartwarming, overcoming heartbreak through God, touches your heart. A worthwhile read for all generations.

A reader: Internet 5 star rating: ***When God Broke Grandma's Heart:*** a must read for all generations. FANTASTIC!

A reviewer Internet 5 star rating: ***When God Took Grandma Home****:* Moves you, captivating.

A reviewer, a Kentucky reader: Internet 5 star rating: ***When God Took Grandma Home****:* MUST READ! Touching story of life's tragedies and how lessons learned from these heartbreaking events can turn into blessings.

Characters

in the novels by Helen Glowacki

Grandma: Grandma's life was filled with sibling betrayal and marital abuse. Her love of God, home remedies and famous boxing stance touches the heart.

Sarah: Sarah helps Grandma write her journal, learns about God's plan of salvation and the enemy who wants to harm her. She carries on Grandma's legacy of faith.

Matt: Matt, Sarah's husband, has a rock-like faith but when he loses a loved one, he struggles with his anger at God, until he has a miraculous experience of faith.

Paul: Paul is Matt's older brother who earned a Captain's license for a seagoing tugboat. His faith sustains him despite enduring terrible circumstances.

Mary and Kevin: Mary and Kevin become Matt and Sarah's neighbors and friends. Mary's panic attacks end when God brings them a miracle they never thought possible.

Elizabeth: Elizabeth adopts Rebecca, loses her husband twelve years later, is confronted with a potentially deadly illness and searches for Rebecca's birth mother.

Rebecca: Rebecca is Elizabeth daughter and Jayden's friend. Her father's death, the illness her mother faces, and a series of challenges at college almost destroy her.

John: John, a deacon in his church, lost his wife to a debilitating disease, becomes Elizabeth's friend, and helps his daughter and grandson through a difficult divorce.

Jayden: Jayden is John's grandson and becomes Rebecca's friend. He has learned that prayer helps solve problems and he and Rebecca begin to share their faith.

Wade and Ruth: Wade is Jim's boss and friend who adopts two children from Iraq. Ruth is Jayden's mother and John's daughter who struggles to let go of the past.

Joshua and Debbie: Joshua, Sarah's younger brother, was demanding and judgmental until Caleb stepped in. Debbie looks to Joshua's family to be her role models.

Caleb and Ann: Caleb is Sarah and Josh's older brother and the family looks to him as they once looked to Grandma. Ann, Caleb's wife harbors a secret sadness.

Barbara and Jim: Barbara, Matt's sister is also Sarah's close friend. Her husband Jim plays devil's advocate in family debates, and matchmaker for his friend Wade.

Heza and Bara: Heza and Bara endured a suicide bomber attack when Bara was one and one half years old and Heza as she was born. They are adopted by Wade.

Chaldeth: Chaldeth is a fallen angel sent to destroy Grandma's family. He plots to bring great heartache to Rebecca and Jayden and their family to break their faith.

Durk: Durk, abused by a cruel father, is a sophomore at the college Rebecca and Jayden attend. He brings harm to Rebecca and Jayden but Jim gives him a second chance.

Professsor T. Nagorra, and Emils, and Dean Peerca: These tenured professors befriend Durk and engage in activities which harm the students and the college campus.

Professors Doog and Sendnik, and President Legna: These three share a faith in God, a love for their country, and desire to be role models. They help save the campus.

Richard and Rachel: Richard is a physician for whom Caleb built a house on the property next door to where he and Ann. live. Both couples share godly values and thus became friends.

Joe and Preacher: Both men work for the company which hired Caleb to supervise the construction of a shopping mall. Preacher wants to teach Joe what scripture says. Joe resists only to tease Preacher.

"One thing have I
desired of the Lord,
that I will seek after;
that I may dwell
in the house of the Lord
all the days of my life,
to behold the beauty
of the Lord,
and to enquire
in his temple."

Psalm 27: 4

www.ingramcontent.com/pod-product-compliance
Lightning Source LLC
LaVergne TN
LVHW092324080426
835508LV00039B/644